Contents

Foreword

The principal reason for keeping pigs is to provide high quality protein foods for humans. Indeed it is forecast that global pig production needs to increase by some 25 per cent in the next twenty years to meet the demands of an expanding human population, and technologies and knowledge must be developed to meet this increasing need.

In this respect, pig production is a dynamic and ever-changing industry, which needs to take account of the many complex interactions that influence the growth and development of the animal. These include genetics, nutrition, health, welfare and the environment, as well as market requirements and public awareness. All of these are discussed in the current book written by Neville Beynon. This book is the second and updated edition of *Pigs – A Guide to Management*, first published in 1990 and which proved very popular. Since then our knowledge of pig production has increased through many major and fascinating developments, especially in the management and production of pigs, and many of these are presented in this publication.

This book is intended for those who wish to know more about the current practices and strategies involved in keeping pigs. It is not meant for 'professionals', although they may find it extremely useful. It is aimed at students, those wishing to know more about pig production, and those starting out in the business, and it is written with this objective in mind. It contains a wealth of practical information covering all aspects from genetics to breeding, growth, nutrition, housing, management and welfare, and carcass and meat quality.

Neville Beynon is well qualified to write such a book since he has worked all his life with pigs, starting on the family farm in Wales and then with major companies, followed by periods in academia at Sharsholt and Berkshire Colleges of Agriculture, the latter as Head of Agriculture. Over the last twenty years he has developed his own consultancy business, N. & R. Services, advising on the management and production of pigs in the UK and abroad.

The broad spectrum of information contained within the pages of this guide provides all the basic facts relevant to the many factors influencing pig production. This will allow practical strategies to be developed to improve pig production in order to meet the needs of a rapidly expanding human population. This book should be on the bookshelf of all those interested in knowing more about pigs.

Dr William H. Close

perception of what is sweet or 'meaty' – although piglets certainly appear to have a sweet tooth. Unfortunately they also have a high tolerance for things containing a lot of salt, and this can be extremely dangerous. Nevertheless, this has led to an ability to consume a range of food sources well beyond the taste range of the human omnivore, and the pig has made good use of this, despite an inability to utilize high-fibre diets as efficiently as ruminants.

Man, the hunter gatherer, must have eaten various forms of wild pig from earliest times. Cave paintings and the discovery of pig bones testify to this. The exact timing and method of the pig's domestication is becoming easier to explain now that we have been able to read the pig's genetic code. Supporting archaeological evidence indicates that domestication may have actually preceded crop growing.

There is also very strong evidence that domestication occurred in places such as China and Europe independently and at about the same time. Until now, there was a considerable problem in obtaining knowledge of the true descent of the domestic pig, let alone the origin of the numerous breeds that have evolved as recently as the past few centuries. The highly adaptable pig probably saw its chance some eight to twelve thousand years ago, and it is now evident that this may have been sometime before our Neolithic ancestors began to farm crops. The arrival of the village settlements in a forest clearing probably provided the ideal conditions for pigs, with their omnivorous eating habits. Acting the role of scavenger, the pig became the refuse collector of old. Some researchers believe the pioneering

European wild boar, Sus scrofa – *telephoto of a shy lone male in a central European forest in 2013.*

pig also played a significant role in clearing the forests and preparing them for pasture suitable for farming sheep and other grazing animals. Domestication may have evolved over four stages. First contact might have been brought about by the pigs' inquisitive scavenging habits and by living close to humans in early settlements. The twenty-first-century citizens of Berlin, Germany, can testify to this, with around 8,000 wild boar living within the city limits in small woodland pockets. They would certainly have found it advantageous to live close to man's new-found village-based food-production industry we now call farming. The second stage may have involved some containment and control of the troublesome pig in order for it to provide useful products. The third stage might have involved the beginnings of husbandry and selection for valued characteristics – for example, wild stock may have been used to breed for size or some other economically important characteristic. By the fourth stage, the wild pig would no longer have contributed to the types that developed into the European and Asian domesticated pigs (*Sus scrofa palustris* and *Sus vittatus*), although it is now known that their genes have had a significant role to play in modern pig breeds. Pigs the exploiters had become the exploited.

It is probable that the Chinese were the earliest pig farmers in the modern sense. Excavations at Zengpiyan, Guilin and Guangxi Zhuang confirmed that pig farming existed there 10,000 years ago. They have had a major influence on the development of pig breeds worldwide, and their breeds, based on the Asian wild pig (*Sus orisatus*) and the sunda pig (*Sus vittatus*), have developed in a unique and diverse style, with some fascinating physical characteristics. The Pig Genome project has also shown that the European wild pig and the Asian wild pig developed separately for about a million years and almost became distinct species. This has all probably added to the tremendous diversity found in the pig's genetic make-up, and in turn the significant variation we find in the 250 or so pig breeds found worldwide.

Pig meat was, and continues to be, the most versatile of meats. As with his cousin the wild boar, the meat, fat, hair, hide, teeth and bones of the domesticated pig provided these early farmers with food, clothing, furniture, decoration, and fat for candles and lamps. Various offals may also have been used for primitive medicines. Insulin (now also synthetically produced), skin graft material and heart valves are just a few modern examples. Archaeologists have linked the presence of large collections of pig bones at Neolithic burial mounds in the UK and Europe (barrows and longmounds) with feasting and high social status settlements. There is little doubt that the pig played a significant and perhaps formerly underestimated part in the social foundations of prehistoric Britain. The pig became important in Britain during the Saxon-Norman period, when poor peasant villages clubbed together to pay for a swineherd. The social status of the swineherd in charge of the domestic pig was never high, and yet, paradoxically, the wild boar was, and is, respected in Europe as the ultimate hunt for the aristocracy.

The pig reached its peak around the Norman Conquest, and then declined due to the restriction on pannage, gradual loss of forests and the rise in importance of sheep. This led to changes in pig husbandry and urged the development of alternatives to grazing acorns and beech mast to systems based on cereals and pulses (peas and beans being fed). These were, and continue to be, expensive commodities, and an imbalance in supply and demand, often caused by harvest failures, meant that pigs were often uneconomical. They began to be housed for longer periods, often on a one per household basis, being fed predominantly on kitchen waste, and this is probably when improvement in pig type began to take place. The traditional swineherd's medieval pig was a lanky, coarse, long-legged and hairy animal, and had features in common with his cousin the wild boar, from whom he was certainly derived. The housed pig was smaller and fatter, similar to the Chinese types.

This suggests that two distinct types of pig existed for many centuries in varying numbers, side by side, and that they were kept in different husbandry systems. There were, of course, considerable

The world's heaviest pig at 1,222kg in 1986, in Taiwan. PIG INTERNATIONAL

regional variations, and the maintenance of pannage rights in areas such as the New Forest helped perpetuate a strain of pig that had the constitution to forage for mast in the forest. In other areas, brewery or dairy by-products led to intensive pig production. In the eighteenth and nineteenth centuries industrial food manufacturers were buying young store pigs in their thousands and droving them to London to fatten them on starch by-products. Thriving droving industries developed; for example, Welsh drovers linked with the dairy regions of Wiltshire, Gloucestershire and Cheshire, and some of these pigs were grown on to produce 'Wiltshire Cure' bacon, considered the best in the country. The economic survival of the Welsh store pig producer therefore depended on the drover, and this interdependence of the weaner producer and his customer, the grower and finisher of slaughter pigs, with the location of slaughter outlets, continues to influence the structure of the pig industry to this day.

The seventeenth century saw the introduction and influence of Chinese and Neapolitan pigs. These were smaller and matured earlier than the Old English types, and the breeding fashion during the mid-nineteenth century led to the extinction of many of the larger breeds in favour of these early maturing types. The old large breeds had been recorded as growing to a massive three-quarters of a ton at two years of age, and had apparently been used exclusively for bacon production.

There were many theories about the true descent of most modern breeds. Until the recent reading of the pig genome there was very little evidence to support them. It is, however, possible to trace the emergence of the Yorkshire breed, which probably, by varying degrees of Chinese influence, developed into the Large White Yorkshire and Small White Yorkshire breeds; these were crossed in turn, and produced the Middle White breed. Certainly at the Royal Show in Birmingham in 1876 there were three distinct categories of the Yorkshire breed of White pig. We can probably thank the apparent love of Yorkshire folk for a monster pig such as the Old Yorkshire, whose genes were maintained in good measure in the Large White breed. That said, the pig genome project confirms that of the twenty-one thousand pig genes that encode protein growth and development, more than a third of them in all UK pig breeds have come from the Asian pigs that were first brought in less than 200 years ago.

As a pure breed, the Large White is probably the most important in the world (especially when the related USA Yorkshire breed is included), though we cannot thank the British farmer for this. The pioneer breeder of Yorkshires, and more specifically the Large White, was a weaver from Keighley, named Joseph Tuley. Apparently such small-scale pig keepers had an enthusiasm for improving pigs matched only by their love of pigeons and greyhound dogs. According to the *Journal of the Royal Agricultural Society of 1881*, by 1850 they had produced a far more refined animal than the coarse mammoth formerly seen in our show yards and now found upon some northern farms.

Unfortunately for many of the larger breeds, the show ring was working against them. The farmer breeders' obsession with fat production, and the smaller cuts demanded by the increasingly affluent consumers, led to a period in British pig breeding which, in retrospect, was clearly based on the wrong priorities and lost opportunities (Julian Wiseman, *see* Further Reading). The London trade demanded a small pork pig of 40 to 70lb (31kg) carcase weight, with no more than 1¼ in (32mm) of fat, whereas the industrial regions, and particularly Birmingham, demanded larger pigs of up to 350lb (155kg); it is interesting to note that the Midlands slaughter weight remained significantly heavier until relatively recently. Apparently, those involved in manual labour and those whose work demanded the consumption of a cold meal preferred larger cuts of meat from heavier pigs. The cottager's pig was often slaughtered at these heavy weights.

Also the development of bacon curing, based on very highly salted meat, was no longer confined to the cold months of the year, and should have inspired the breeders to produce larger, leaner pigs. This was because George Harris of Calne, in Wiltshire, had discovered an American curing process that could be carried out throughout the summer using an ice-cooled house. In 1864, together with his brother Thomas, he patented and perfected a mild cure (Wiltshire Cure) which did not require a large fat covering to take up the salt essential in hard-salt (dry) cure.

Wiltshire sides of bacon cured on the farm in an outhouse.

But the breeders, for some reason, probably associated with the 'fancy' of the show ring, applied the wrong priorities, and lost opportunities that were staring them in the face. Neither pork nor bacon production required fat pigs, yet the breeders continued to consider a good 'breeding pig' to be essentially fat. Charles Spencer stated *c.* 1880 that the sheep judges had the additional responsibility of judging pigs, and 'they generally put the Middle Whites first because their nice square backs used to appeal to the sheep connoisseur'. It is little wonder that the British pig industry receded whilst the foreign competitors, the USA and Denmark, took over their market. In the event, small fat breeds such as the Small White were to suffer extinction before World War I was over. The Berkshire breed managed to make some rapid improvement and survives to this day, although, along with the Middle White, it is a threatened, rare breed.

In 1884, the National Pig Breeders' Association (NPBA – now the BPA and NPA) was founded, based on three British breeds of pedigree pig: the Large White, the Middle White and the Tamworth. The Association's chief aim in those days was to set standards for breeders and to assist in the improvement of UK swine. It is interesting to note that by the time the first herd book was published on 1 May 1885, the pedigree registers included Berkshires, Blacks and Small Whites. Not all breeds had developed societies at this time, and even when formed, they often worked separately, a situation that has persisted until relatively recently.

The NPBA was very much involved in the importation of the Landrace in 1949 and the early 1950s. Curiously, this breed came from Sweden, not Denmark. The Danes had sold Landrace pigs to

The small White c. *1910.*

Vietnamese pot-bellied pigs, now often sold as pet 'micro-pigs'.
MATTHEW CURRAN

Chinese Fengiing pig with thirty-nine piglets. This breed belongs to the same Taihu breed group as the Meishan pig. FAO

Canada, and because these had failed to perform well, the British Government looked to Sweden, where the Landrace was also well developed. Once again it is a peculiarity that the Landrace breeders ran their own herd book right up to 1978 when the Landrace Breed Society finally merged with the NPBA.

In the 1950s the NPBA was instrumental in the setting up of pig testing stations designed to provide UK breeders with their first scientific breeding scheme. This led to the setting up of the Pig Industry Development Authority (PIDA), which in turn became the basis for the Meat and Livestock Commission (MLC). The MLC still operates services for the meat sector, but the British Pig Executive (BPEX) now continues to provide excellent advisory and consultancy services to the pig industry.

From 1982 the NPBA also evolved into a trade organization representing commercial producers' interests and forming an effective pressure group. It was renamed the BPA in 1991. The roles were split in 1998 when the NFU Pigs Committee also joined and merged to form the National Pig Association (NPA). The NPA took on its role as the sole trade industry body, and the British Pig Association retained its role representing British pig breeders at home and abroad, maintaining the pedigree herd books and having a central role in helping to prevent breeds becoming extinct. This is an essential task, supported by the Rare Breeds Survival Trust, because many of our native traditional breeds have fewer than 500 sows left in the UK.

In 2013 the British Pig Association represents fourteen breeds: the Berkshire, British Saddleback, Duroc, Gloucester Old Spot, Hampshire, British Landrace, Large Black, Large White, Mangalitza, Middle White, Oxford Sandy and Black, Pietrain, Tamworth and Welsh.

PIG NUMBERS

World pork production was predicted by the FAO to reach a record of 112 million metric tons in 2012. In 2011 it was estimated that China alone produced about 50 million tons of pig meat and had a pig population of more than 466 million. The next largest was the USA with more than 10 million tons from a total population of 60 million pigs. Asia Pacific accounted for 57 per cent of all pig meat output in 2011. The world total census of pigs is probably about one billion, and close to half of these are found in China. The figures show that China has some way to go to catch up the USA and other nations on productivity, but they are doing so, and this will result in more pig meat produced more efficiently and economically from the same number of breeding pigs. It is interesting to note that although the number of sows in the USA was 20 per cent smaller than in 1991, the pig meat output in 2012 was expected to be 35 per cent more than in 1991. This has resulted in pig meat being produced at a lower cost relative to earlier times, coupled with rapid increases in consumption in developing economies. There is, and always has been, a strong positive link between world economic and population growth and that of pig meat consumption.

Over the 130-year period from the mid-1880s there has been a marked increase in pig production with big variations in developments between countries. The British count has gone from 2.62 million then to about 4.5 million today, although in 1883 James Long suggested that there were probably another million pigs at that time, kept by cottagers and town labourers, for which there was no count. The cottager's pig was a common feature well into the 1950s, when it finally disappeared – the important role it played in the household economy and nutrition of the working classes in both town and country had all but gone by the middle of the twentieth century.

The maximum number of pigs in the UK peaked in about 1998 at around 8.1 million, and the recent decline illustrates the rapid change in the sow herd that occurred by the middle of the last decade due to severe economic pressure, largely the result of two notifiable disease episodes in 2000 and 2001 (swine fever and foot and mouth), exacerbated by expensive unilateral new sow housing welfare regulations for the UK breeding herd in 1999. The UK sow stall ban was strictly implemented, whilst their EU counterparts were able to continue with lower cost confinement systems until 2013, when a partial ban (after the first four weeks of gestation) was meant to be enforced across all EU states. The survival of any pig industry will ultimately

The Danish 'Danbred' sow is currently one of the most successful 'hyper-prolific' dam-line hybrid sows, with top performing herds successfully rearing approaching thirty-five piglets reared and weaned to four weeks of age per sow per annum. Highly productive and cost-efficient pig production in other countries will pose an ongoing threat and challenge to the UK pig producer. DANISH AGRICULTURAL COUNCIL

depend on economics, and in particular currency exchange rates, and this will often relate back directly to political decision making that affects trade, the competitiveness of the home industry, and maintaining good biosecurity against imported diseases.

Wars have devastating effects on society and all industries. The pig can be seen to compete with the human population for food when there is a scarcity, such as that created during a world war: thus in 1914 there were 2.5 million pigs, while in 1918 there were 1.75 million; similarly in 1938 there were 3.5 million pigs and in 1945 there were 1.5 million. Immediately after World War II it was clear that untold damage had been done to UK pig meat quality. During that period of food rationing and up until 1953 when the government decontrolled the pig meat market, the War Agricultural Executive had operated a flat rate price policy with no regard for quality. Cheap bulky feeds including boiled potatoes and swill (kitchen and canteen waste) had been used, with little or no regard for balanced pig diets.

Attempts were made in the 1930s to operate national pig-buying contracts for bacon manufacture, though these had already failed before the outbreak of war due to a lack of market discipline. Suggestions that Britain should set up pig-breeding testing stations were made in the 1920s, but these were to take another thirty years to materialize. The Danes had already been breeding pigs scientifically for seventy years when the first British pig progeny testing station finally opened in 1958. However, British researchers led the world, and the work of Sir John Hammond provided the basis for understanding growth and development in pigs. This laid the foundations for much of the highly successful and profitable work that came to fruition in the 1950s and 1960s, and which has been successfully carried forward into the future.

In 1953 free market forces began to function once again, and soon over-production of low quality pigs depressed the market, resulting in a steady reduction in the number of pig herds due to a lack of profitability. However, successful herds began to increase in size with the application of up-to-date breeding and production methods, and the importation of the Swedish Landrace in 1949 and 1953 made a dramatic impact on all UK breeds. The Welsh breed opened up its herd book for a period in the mid-1950s and allowed the use of pure Landrace blood. The photograph of our Champion Welsh boar and Reserve Supreme Champion at the 1951 Royal Welsh Show was typical of the shape and conformation of the old Welsh breed, but the Landrace infusion changed the pig dramatically, and by the late 1950s it was very different, retaining the sound constitution and

The old Welsh type before the Landrace influence; exhibited by D. V. Beynon at the Royal Welsh Show in 1951.

ROYAL WELSH SHOW 1951
RESERVE SUPREME CHAMPION
CHAMPION WELSH BOAR

GLANTAF NODWR 3rd

The modern Welsh breed.

hardiness of the old Welsh breed, but combining these qualities with the improved carcase quality and production efficiency of the scientifically bred Landrace. It is interesting to note that recent discoveries within the pig genome have shown that the genes that produced an increase in the number of vertebrae and extra ribs in these longer pigs originally came from the European wild boar (*Sus scrofa*).

The hybrid pig-breeding industry came into existence in the late 1950s when a number of today's highly successful and now frequently multi-national breeding companies were formed. The Wall's Meat Company (Unilever) developed its hybrid pig scheme in 1958, followed closely by a group of farmers in the Thames Valley who set up the now multinational Pig Improvement Company (PIC). British pig-breeding companies have made, and continue to make, significant contributions to pig breeding and its associated technology across the world. During the mid-1970s there were twenty-eight UK-based breeding companies listed through the NPBA and carrying out pig-testing programmes. Independent pedigree breeders took part in the early PIDA (Pig Industry Development Authority – *see* page 14) breeding schemes, which were maintained until relatively recently by the Meat and Livestock Commission.

During these early years Dr Melrose of the MAFF (Ministry of Agriculture, Fisheries and Food) breeding centre at Shinfield developed commercially viable artificial insemination techniques, including the now internationally used Melrose reusable rubber spiral pig insemination catheter, which is also available in a disposable model. Despite an early start (1955) with a considerable boost in the mid-1960s when Wall's and MLC began to develop their commercial pig artificial insemination schemes, the number of pig inseminations in the UK only really began to expand significantly during the late 1980s when the other large breeding companies began to encourage its use. Pig AI is now used widely and good results are consistently achieved on commercial farms, with world class support from the breeding companies and organizations such as BPEX (British Pig Executive – *see* page 14).

TYPES OF MODERN PIG PRODUCER

There are a number of different types of pig farming business, and these are typical for UK situations, as described below.

The weaner producer: Breeds and sells weaner or store pigs from an indoor or outdoor unit. For example, in 2013 approaching 40 per cent of UK sows are kept on outdoor breeding units, and piglets weaned at the end of their fourth week are often sold directly from the field to specialist weaner-rearer and finishing units. (In 2012 fewer than 3 per cent of pigs were reared to slaughter weight outdoors.)

Breeder, weaner – grower – finishing herds: These producers either operate on one site, or have the breeding herd housed at a different location to the weaner rearing herd. It is not uncommon for the finishing herd to be on a third site within the same farming business – a so-called 'split-site' arrangement. This breeding herd can be based outdoors, as well as the weaner rearing stage. However, finishing pigs to slaughter weight outdoors is not common because they require excessive amounts of feed and demand a much higher premium price at slaughter.

Finishing herds: These producers buy in weaner pigs (at 7kg plus) or the heavier 'grower' pigs (at 35kg) and rear them to sell at commercial slaughter weights – now normally around 105kg live weight and increasing, with typical average carcase weights at around 80kg.

The pedigree producer: Breeds and sells breeding pigs, maintains rare breeds and pedigree lines (male and female); such concerns are often sensibly combined with either selling the meat products directly to the consumer, or supplying the local farmers' markets or farm shops.

Breeding stock multiplication units: The production of breeding stock on contract to, or run by, commercial breeding companies – known as multiplication herds. This usually involves producing breeding gilts from so-called 'grandparent stock' (GP and GGP) using semen and/or breeding stock supplied from the breeding company's nucleus herds.

The breeding company: These companies usually operate throughout the world with specialist pig units involved within a so-called highly integrated pig-breeding pyramid. They also offer AI direct to the commercial pig keeper, along with serving their own multiplication and nucleus herds. They provide hybrid breeding gilts from

UK pig herd down in December and at lowest level in more than 60 years

Million head

The size of the UK pig herd, prepared and commented on by BPEX (AHDB) 2012. Source: Agricultural census data taken from 'A hundred years of British Food & Farming' until 1983, and the devolved UK national agriculture departments from 1984 onwards.

specialist dam lines bred for outdoor and indoor herds, specialist market outlets and hyper-prolific breeding lines, along with a range of matching 'meat line' boars (usually hybrids) for natural service or AI.

Pig numbers in the UK peaked during the last third of the twentieth century, but since the millennium there has been a steady fall for the reasons listed earlier. The current numbers are half of what they were and almost the lowest in living memory. This clearly illustrates the tough economic and political reality facing the modern pig producer, just as it has done throughout history.

2

The Market and its Influence on Breeds and Systems

The days when it was considered unsafe to eat pork if there was not an 'r' in the month are long gone now that we have the universal distribution of the domestic refrigerator. Pig meat is the most versatile of all meats, marketed as fresh pork, bacon, ham and other added value products such as pâté, sausages and pies. In Britain, however, the level of self-sufficiency in these products has fallen with the decline in the pig breeding herd.

About one-third of the total 27kg of pig meat consumed per annum by the average Briton is eaten as bacon, one quarter fresh pork and approaching half as processed pig meat. Pig meat consumption in Britain rose by around 17 per cent during the 1980s, whilst bacon had to fight to maintain its place. In fact bacon consumption declined rapidly following Britain's entry into the European Community in 1972, prior to which bacon consumption was around 11.5kg per person, per year, as compared to 8kg in the late 1980s. The annual per capita consumption levels for pig meat in the EU in 2012 are shown in the accompanying diagram.

The following table provides an overview of pig meat consumption in the UK in 2011. There has been a significant increase in processed pig meat products sold over the past twenty-five years.

The UK has a below average consumption of pig meat, but has an above EU average consumption for all meats. We consume close to 30kg of poultry meat, 25kg pig meat, 22kg beef and about 6kg of lamb per person per year. It is interesting to note that in 2011, 82 per cent of bacon and pork sales were made through the large UK supermarkets. The total amount of pig meat consumed in the UK remains close to an impressive 1.25 million tons per annum.

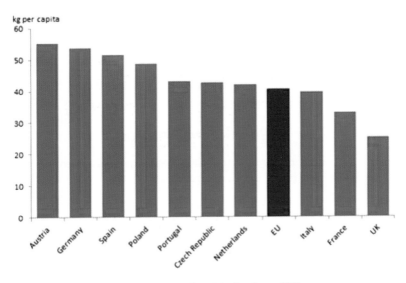

Per capita pig meat consumption in selected EU Member States, 2012.

UK Pig Meat Consumption as Bacon, Pork and Processed Products

	Bacon	Pork	Processed
% Sales	33.3%	22.4%	44.3%
British	126,000	199,000	151,000
Imported	280,000	74,000	389,000
Total	406,000	273,000	540,000
Self-sufficiency %	31.0%	72.9%	28.0%

QUALITY IN PIG MEAT PRODUCTION

Modern consumers demand lean meat with little visible fat; they care about its appearance and texture, and demand it in a form that is easy to cook and to serve cold, and is good to eat. There has been a dramatic reduction in the fat content of pig carcases over the past half century, and the average British pork pig is now leaner than many broiler chickens. Pork, like chicken, is also lower in the saturated fats associated with high cholesterol than other so-called red meats and dairy products.

The tremendous reduction in pig carcase fat content has been achieved by a combination of genetic selection, nutritional manipulation and fine tuning by the producer, encouraged by the strict carcase classification pig payment schemes. Carcase classification is based on measuring fat depth and lean meat content. On 1 January 1989 the EEC introduced a new Pig Carcase Classification Scheme for all abattoirs slaughtering more than two hundred pigs. This reports an estimated lean meat content based on a six-point scale – SEUROP – where 'S' is the best and 'P' the worst.

Abattoirs in Britain use various devices to take these measurements, including the long-established optical probe, which is operated by reading the fat depth at precise and defined positions over

Standard optical probe for P2 and P1 + P3 measurement.

MLC operator and electronic probe.

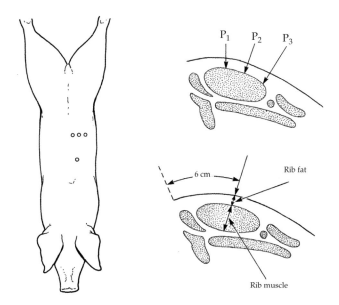

Location of probing sites on a pig carcase.

the eye muscle at the head of the last rib. The diagram defines the positions, and the photographs illustrate the method employed. The optical viewfinder blade is inserted into the carcase at probe position (P1 and P3 or P2 only). The fat depth is measured with the barrel adjusted with the viewfinder sight glass centre wire sight directly on the lean and fat line. The fat depth is then read off the measuring barrel.

A number of abattoirs have invested in automatic probes that calculate lean meat content. These probes are also used to measure fat depth over the eye muscle, but because of slightly different designs in the probe shafts (blades), the positions may differ and include more readings. The most advanced versions involve sophisticated scanning and computer technology.

Consumers are becoming increasingly concerned with the possible presence of residues in meat and the traceability of the product through from farm to table. Hormones were banned in pig meat production in the late 1970s, long before the ban in other meats, and there are no anabolic steroids implicated in pig meat production in the EU. Food scares and corrupt practices have increased the consumers' wish to buy locally produced foods.

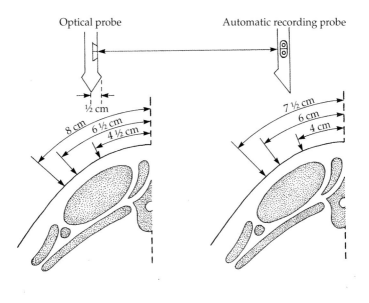

Location of probe measuring windows and probe insertion points.

Consumer concerns have provided marketing opportunities, and organically produced pig meat and high welfare, real pork-producing companies have traded successfully, commanding a healthy financial premium for their niche products. Wild boar has also been on offer from British herds through specialist outlets since the 1980s. There is clearly an opportunity for the pig industry to develop a healthy eating image for its many products and to break into new markets, with the emphasis on UK-produced pig meat under schemes such as the 'Red Tractor' logo, which guarantees traceability back to the farm and through the pork chain to the consumer, with high levels of welfare being monitored throughout.

PSE AND DFD MEAT QUALITY PROBLEMS

Pale soft exudative (wet) or PSE meat is a problem related to very lean pigs, and in particular, to breeds and strains that carry the so-called halothane gene, which also causes porcine stress syndrome;

it is therefore also known as the PSS gene. Pigs that carry this gene tend to run a higher risk of sudden death during periods of stress, such as during transport from farm to farm or to the abattoir. Breeders can detect the gene by using halothane gas, but since the 1990s a quick, simple and accurate DNA test has been available. Using the gas, those carrying the gene react positively by becoming extremely stiff, and prolonged treatment with halothane would lead to heart failure, whereas pigs that are halothane negative merely go to sleep peacefully in a relaxed state. DNA tests are now generally used instead of halothane.

There is strong link between meat with a higher lean content and the PSS gene. Some breeds, such as the British Large White, are almost free of the gene, whilst the traditional original Belgian Pietrain breed was in the past recorded with 88 per cent positive reactors. Modern pig-breeding programmes have now successfully limited the negative effects of the PSS gene whilst maintaining the potential for excellent lean meat growth.

Dark, firm, dry meat, or DFD, is also caused by stress, but it is of a different nature. This problem occurs if animals have been fighting for long periods, perhaps after mixing at the slaughter house in the holding area (known as the lairage); the same thing happens when bulls are mixed for long periods prior to slaughter. DFD is quite simply muscle that has almost run out of blood sugar, the animals being at the point of exhaustion when slaughtered. Many such meat quality issues occur between the pig leaving the farm and prior to the meat being chilled after slaughter.

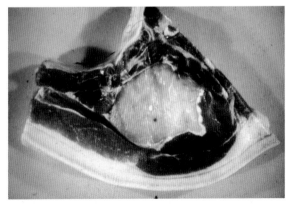

PSE muscle in a pork chop.

The Autofatometer measures the carcase using an array of probes that measure the carcase fat and lean at multiple sites whilst the carcase travels over them. The data is processed immediately by computer, and the various carcase cuts (primal cuts) can be selected for specific requirements.

Automatic cutting and sorting of pig carcase cuts based on computer scanning in a Danish cutting plant. DANISH AGRICULTURAL COUNCIL

Marbling of Fat within Lean Meat

The Duroc pig has been hailed as the breed that can put succulence back into commercially produced pork. As back fat levels have declined, so too has the intramuscular fat content, but it is claimed that some breeds have higher levels of this fat within the meat. Marbling is a web of fat running through the muscle. The Duroc breed has continued to become very lean but has maintained high marbling at low P2 fat depth. The Duroc also has high levels of polyunsaturated fatty acid. The Tamworth, in contrast, has low marbling at greater P2 fat depths and contains higher levels of saturated fats.

Marbling within the lean meat is considered highly desirable in Japan, and both Berkshire and Middle White pigs have found preference there for this reason. It is clearly no longer accurate to link marbling with a fatter type of pig, and it remains to be seen if it really is possible to reduce back fat considerably whilst maintaining a reasonable amount of marbling in commercial slaughter pigs.

There is considerable interest in producing more succulent meat, even if the end product is more expensive. This demands genetic selection for this trait as well as fine tuning and manipulating the pig's diet. However, as has been stated, appropriate treatment of the pigs at slaughter and care of the carcase are also factors that influence the succulence and eating quality of the meat.

MEAT INSPECTION AND LICENSED SLAUGHTER PREMISES

All abattoirs must have a meat inspector who checks every carcase to confirm that it is fit for human consumption. Slaughtering may only be carried out on licensed premises by licensed slaughterers. High standards for licensing slaughterhouses are legislated for in the EU, and this is essential for export purposes (including intra-community trade).

MARKETS FOR FINISHED PIGS

At the time of writing in 2013 the UK market for pigs is basically for pigs destined for bacon curing (now often for only part of the carcase), and so-called 'cutter pigs', which are cut into 'primal' joints for sale both as fresh or frozen pork cuts and for processing into various processed products. The traditional range of slaughter weights, classes and names still apply, apart from the heavy hog, but the heavy cutter

Name	Live weight	Carcase weight (kg)	Killing or dressing out (%)
Pork	60–75	44–55	73+
Light cutter	75–82	55–60	74+
Cutter	80–93	60–70	75+
Bacon	80–106	60–82	77+
Heavy cutter	85–118	65–95	77+
Heavy hog	90–128	70–100	78+

pig is now increasingly slaughtered within the weight range of the traditional heavy hog. The average weight of a GB-finished pig carcase is around 78 to 80kg in 2013. However, they are often up to 2kg lighter on average in the summer months.

The table above provides a reasonable example of the weight ranges and pig types at slaughter, along with example carcase weights and killing out percentage values. Most pigs are paid for at a dressed carcase weight, as defined in the national or EU grading scheme. With pigs, the dressed carcase weight includes the head and feet after the pluck and digestive system have been removed; the tongue may or may not be included, but must be allowed for in the estimated cold carcase weight.

It is important to note that pigs, like other slaughter animals, have an improved dressing out percentage as they grow heavier. In general, it can also be stated that ad-lib fed and/or fatter pigs kill out by up to two percentage points higher than restricted and/or very lean pigs from the traditional breeds. Entire male pigs tend to dress out by up to 1 per cent less than their female or castrated counterparts. There are also breed differences; for example, the very lean 'blocky' European breeds and hybrid boar sire-line progeny dress out better than the traditional UK white breeds.

Entire Male Slaughter Pigs

The majority of male pigs in the UK are no longer castrated and are sold as so-called 'entires'. They are leaner than their castrated brothers and convert feed more efficiently, but there are some negative aspects: for example, there is a slightly different distribution of muscle – there is more on the shoulder – and a higher incidence of fat quality problems, although their meat contains less saturated fat. There are also problems where fat separates from the lean in carcases with thin back fat cover, and the rind can be damaged because of fighting between boars and sexual activity as they reach puberty.

The risk of 'taint' is present: this is a smell based on the male pig musk (sex odour, androsterone), released from the fat on cooking; however, it is currently not taken as a serious problem in the UK, although as we move to heavier slaughter weights the pigs will be older and the risk may increase. Electronic equipment that can detect this boar taint odour is now available, and is often fitted to meat plants. There is a secondary cooking smell problem, which also occurs in gilts and hogs, although it is possibly worse in entire males, caused by the faint odour of an aromatic substance called skatole.

If pigs were sold at the heavier European weights, androsterone could lead to increased taint problems. Welfare legislation is planned to come into force in the EU that will restrict the practice of surgical castration by January 2018. A vaccine is available that inhibits the release of hormones in the young boar, which in turn suppresses the production of androsterone. It should also be remembered that too much fish meal and other feed ingredients of this type can cause a major smell and taste problem in the end product.

Experts within the pig industry in the UK advise a move towards a heavier national average slaughter weight, which is seen as desirable on economic and marketing grounds. It does make sense as the weaner cost is shared over more kilograms. However, the ultimate decision has to be based on the total cost of producing a kilogram of carcase commensurate to the price received from the market. The following average carcase weights highlight the considerable difference between selected European countries and the lighter average weight of pigs sold in the UK and Ireland.

Average Carcase Weights in Different European Countries in 2011 (kg)

Italy	127
Belgium	94
France	81
West Germany	94
Netherlands	92
Denmark	82
Ireland	80
UK	80

Note: The average UK carcase weight has risen rapidly since 2000, and by at least 15kg over the past thirty years.
Source: EU/FAO data.

Types of Slaughter Pig Carcase

Italy has a traditional product in the form of the large Parma hams that are air-dry salt cured in northern Italy; this demands carcases above 130kg. The UK market for pig meat is also quite complex in that the traditional pork butcher now only trades a very small, but still significant part of the fresh pork market, whilst the large retail business trades in primal cuts that are frequently pre-packed and labelled for sale in the meat plant.

Fewer so-called bacon pigs are now wholly cured into traditional sides. The shoulders and sometimes the hams are removed for

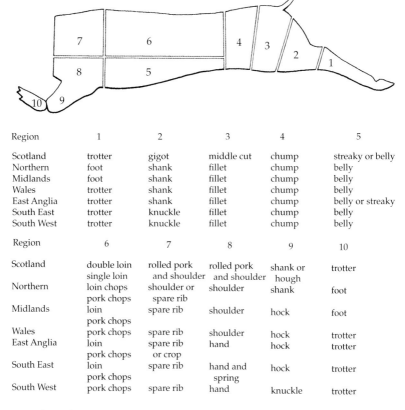

Region	1	2	3	4	5
Scotland	trotter	gigot	middle cut	chump	streaky or belly
Northern	foot	shank	fillet	chump	belly
Midlands	foot	shank	fillet	chump	belly
Wales	trotter	shank	fillet	chump	belly
East Anglia	trotter	shank	fillet	chump	belly or streaky
South East	trotter	knuckle	fillet	chump	belly
South West	trotter	knuckle	fillet	chump	belly

Region	6	7	8	9	10
Scotland	double loin single loin	rolled pork and shoulder	rolled pork and shoulder	shank or hough	trotter
Northern	loin chops pork chops	shoulder or spare rib	shoulder	shank	foot
Midlands	loin pork chops	spare rib	shoulder	hock	foot
Wales	pork chops	spare rib	shoulder	hock	trotter
East Anglia	loin pork chops	spare rib or crop	hand	hock	trotter
South East	loin pork chops	spare rib	hand and spring	hock	trotter
South West	pork chops	spare rib	hand	knuckle	trotter

Cuts of British pork.

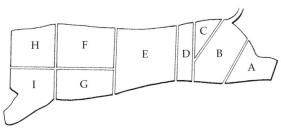

A	Gammon hock	D	Long back (rashers)	G	Prime streaky (rashers)
B	Middle gammon	E	Middle or throughcut (rashers)	H	Prime collar
C	Corner gammon	F	Prime back (rashers or chops)	I	Prime forehock

Cuts of British bacon.

alternative products and fresh pork cuts, and many parts of the pig
are exported because we do not have a market for them. In turn the
UK needs almost three times as many hams and pork loins than are
produced from our own pigs. The pig meat market is therefore now
truly international, and this trend will continue.

'The Pork Cuts range'. BPEX

There has been a rapid fall in the traditional market in the UK for roast pork from the smaller pork pig with 'crackling'. A heavier version of these can still be seen hanging as a whole carcase or as 'sides' in the traditional butcher's shop, but at weights above 60kg these days. These butchers prefer gilt carcases because they have no scrotal damage and have finer shoulders. However, these account for a reduced share of the fresh pork market.

The banning of swill feeding as a result of the 2001 foot and mouth disease epidemic brought about the final demise of the heavy hog weight range of finishing pig. Pigs of this slaughter weight were traditionally fed using relatively low cost feeds that are no longer available or no longer permitted because of the risk of importing diseases in meat products (swill feeding). At the other extreme, the small connoisseur market for suckling pig killed and eaten whole, usually between 10 and 20kg live weight, will always have to cover the relatively high cost of the weaner pig.

As a rough guide, the meat from a suckling pig would cost up to three times that from a light pork pig, with very light traditional

UK Market demand in pig numbers for different carcase cuts in 2011

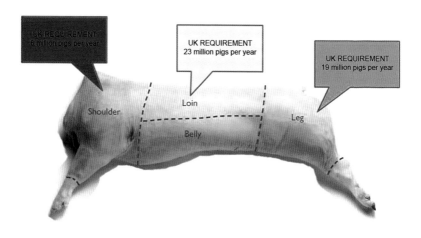

UK pig demand in 2011. UK production is approximately 9 million pigs per year. Adapted from 'Bringing home the bacon', CRESC Public Interest Report 2012.

London 50kg pork pigs requiring a price about 10 to 15% more per kilogram than a modern cutter pig. The lighter cutter pig also requires a higher price per kg to cover the cost of production, as compared to a bacon weight pig. A significant part of our 'pork' exports are accounted for by the 45 per cent of all sows in the UK that are culled annually. A high proportion of their valuable meat is exported to Germany and some other EU countries as manufacturing meat. Some may return to the UK in added value processed delicatessen products.

Despite this low self-sufficiency, UK exports of pig meat (pork) are worth in excess of £250 million per annum. UK pig meat and carcase products are exported to places like China; in 2013 Australia was also importing high value, UK-sourced primal cuts. The restored high health status of British farm animals is central to this, and must be maintained. In some instances it has taken over a decade to regain this status, following the importation of swine fever and foot and mouth disease in contaminated meat at the turn of the twenty-first century. The bottom line is never to feed pigs meat products, regardless of whether they are cooked or not – it is illegal and extremely dangerous.

BRITISH PIG BREEDS

It is now an essential business requirement for the majority of commercial farms to purchase their breeding stock from the breeding companies and independent breeders who are continually improving the genetic potential of their pigs. Many of the hybrid breeding pig lines contain genes that were originally derived from the Large White, Landrace and Welsh breeds, amongst others. These were then selectively bred to provide the great grandparents (GGP) lines in their cross-breeding programmes. Despite this, even the traditional pedigree Large White is now a minority breed.

The Duroc, Hampshire and Pietrain are examples of special purpose pigs, used chiefly in hybrid pig-breeding programmes. A good example is the Duroc, which has, for example, been used to produce special-purpose hybrid sows for outdoor herds. Chinese breeds of the Taihu types, including the Meishan, have also been included in the gene make-up of some hybrid dam lines, for example the Maidan.

The Rare Breeds Survival Trust has a 'Pigs Watchlist' for the original British breeds: the British Lop, the Large Black and the Middle White are listed as 'vulnerable', whilst the Berkshire, Tamworth and Welsh are 'at risk'; the British Saddleback, Gloucester Old Spot,

Large White and Oxford Sandy and Black are all classified as 'minority' breeds. The Mangalitza is a breed that originated in Hungary and neighbouring countries. There are also those breeds kept as pets or for their interest and as an attraction; these include the Vietnamese Pot Bellied and KuneKune. 'Iron Age' pigs are usually Tamworth × wild boar.

The vast majority of sows are now hybrid or cross-bred and have the advantage of larger litter sizes both born and reared. This is due to a phenomenon known as hybrid vigour (heterosis), which boosts

The Large White. Traditionally the most popular 'sire line' boar in the UK.

The Rattlerow boar is an example of an excellent modern hybrid boar with a proportion of genes originating from the Large White combined with a blocky meat type GP meat line.
RATTLEROW FARMS LTD

The Landrace.

The Welsh.

The Middle White.

The Oxford Sandy and Black.

The Duroc.

The Hampshire.

The Berkshire.

The British Saddleback.

The Large Black.

The Tamworth.

The Gloucester Old Spot.

The British Lop.

The Mangalitza.

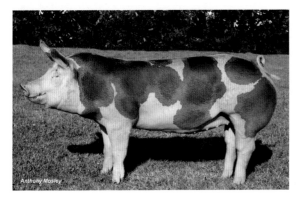

The Pietrain.

the performance of cross-bred offspring beyond that of both parents, or certainly the average of both parents. The degree of improvement depends on the characteristic. Litter size and breeding ability are boosted with around a 10 per cent improvement in numbers reared and heavier piglet weights. Crossing three breeds produces a slightly better improvement than back-crossing or criss-crossing a two breed cross.

Sows and gilts are often culled due to infertility, lameness, rearing performance, temperament and age. One boar is sufficient for about twenty sows in indoor herds not using AI, whilst in outdoor herds it will be nearer ten sows per boar where no AI is used. Indoor herds need about two or three young replacement

The KuneKune.

Anthony Mosley

boars per annum per hundred sows, compared to four to six outdoors. When AI is used for all services, the requirement is mainly for small numbers of 'teaser' (sometimes vasectomized) and 'catch' boars.

It is essential to consider the health status of the source herd, and the following are examples likely to be encountered:

- SPF: specific pathogen-free herds – tend to be within nucleus herds
- HHS: High Health Status (also known as MD, or minimal disease) herds
- Pig Health Scheme (PHS) herds, or Pig Health Control Association and normal health status herds

Take veterinary advice on all purchases and proceed carefully. At the very least put animals purchased from any source into quarantine for a minimum of twenty-eight days, and/or observe the Animal Movement Regulation requirements in force. Always arrange for a specialist veterinary surgeon to check the animals over, treating lice and mange (not usually necessary with SPF pigs), and worm them prior to introduction to the main herd. The vaccination status and treatment requirement of all bought-in replacements is also increasingly important.

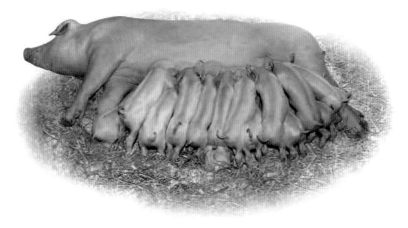

Rattlerow Whiteland (Large White × Landrace) sow and litter. Whiteland sows are already achieving thirty-three pigs born alive/sow/year in 2013. RATTLEROW FARMS LTD

GENETIC MERIT

The boars and gilts purchased as replacements for a commercial breeding herd directly affect the future financial success or otherwise of the farming business. The female breeding stock and the boars selected must be suited to the environment on the unit and have the constitution, temperament, longevity and robustness to achieve top class fertility and rearing results. The piglets produced must have the potential to convert feed efficiently into high quality slaughter pigs as demanded by the meat trade. Outdoor gilts must combine this ability with a constitution that is adaptable in the ever-changing and challenging conditions of the outdoor unit.

These are all examples of traits, along with those of the boar or sire line, selected for their meat-producing potential. All of these traits define the genetic merit of the chosen breeding stock. Breeding stock are selected based on their performance, and with increasingly full reference to each pig or breeding line's unique genetic make-up using DNA analytical techniques and gene mapping. This genomic selection procedure will become increasingly significant and speed up selective breeding. Physical assessment has also long involved the use of technology in the form of ultrasonic measurements designed to assess the individual fat and lean meat content and meat-producing potential of the pig being tested.

The emphasis of this genetic selection will differ between the dam and sire line hybrid breeding pyramids. The dam line must ensure that the breeding sows and gilts are prolific breeders, and have the increased potential to produce and rear consistently large, viable and healthy litters of pigs. These pigs will also inherit the ability to grow lean meat efficiently from both parents, but the emphasis for this is placed on the specially bred 'sire line' or 'meat line' parent boars. There is nothing new in this concept, and the sheep industry has long practised this crossbreeding approach, albeit traditionally crossing native breeds. Both approaches rely on combining characteristics from specialist lines and breeds. Crossbreeding also makes full use of the boost in performance (heterosis) derived from the mixing of genes from distinct and unrelated breeds or lines.

The sequencing of the pig genome has opened up some exciting new possibilities for enhancing selective genomic-based breeding. This new tool will need to be used with great care, but like all new developments, it has the potential to make a positive contribution.

Sophisticated computer programs using techniques such as BLUP (Best Linear Unbiased Prediction) and the prediction of EBVs (Estimated Breeding Values) have long ensured that genetic progress is maintained. This approach is based on estimating the superiority of performance of a boar or gilt over their contemporaries. This will include the following performance factors: daily live weight gain (in grams per day), food conversion efficiency, back fat depth (P1+ P3 in mm) and estimated carcase lean content (per cent). The very best boars are then made available through AI, and the pricing of boars for natural mating can also be influenced by their own performance index. It is not really possible to compare boars from other breeding companies or independent breeders, even if given an EBV

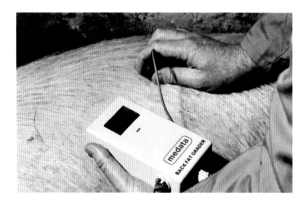

MEDATA back fat measuring device.

or performance index; this can only be facilitated if animals from different sources are tested under the same conditions, a point not always fully understood by many successful pig keepers. Female replacements may also be group tested for growth, and back-fat data measured by ultrasonic tests. In addition, an index can be calculated for home-reared gilts in a pedigree herd based on their live-weight gain, weight for age and ultrasonic back-fat measurements. The additional tool of genomic selection will hopefully aim to produce well developed, healthy, profitable pigs that can enjoy a high welfare lifespan.

VISUAL AND PHYSICAL APPRAISAL

In addition to selection based on performance and genetic markers, the conformation of both boars and gilts must also be appraised by sight and touch. It is important to ensure that the animals conform to type (or breed, if pedigree), and are physically well equipped for the role of breeding as a sow or boar. This should apply even when replacement stock is bought in, and animals failing to match up to acceptable standards should be refused entry into the herd. There is a high wastage rate in sows, and this may well be down to replacements being poorly equipped in the first place.

In examining home-bred and/or bought-in replacement gilts and young boars, the legs and claws deserve particular attention. They should have a streamlined bone structure, stand reasonably straight with legs set at each corner, and be free of bumps or swellings (callouses). The claws should be reasonably even and show no evidence of twisting the leg; the pasterns should be strong and the claws should stand level. Avoid animals that stand excessively on tiptoe or down on their pasterns; they should move and walk easily and be free of stiffness and/or lameness.

The teats also deserve special attention. There is a minimum requirement of six (three pairs), evenly spaced, in front of the navel in gilts (or sheath in the boar). If there are eight teats in front of the navel, this can be a good sign, provided they are evenly spaced. During suckling it is the forward teats that are both most popular and most productive in milk supply. Pigs will have anything from twelve to eighteen teats, with odd numbers as common as even. The BPA requires at least twelve potentially functional teats before an animal may be registered as pedigree. In practice this should be the absolute minimum, and fourteen to sixteen are desirable, because not all will be functional. Some Chinese breeds have twenty functional teats.

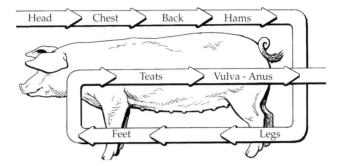

Examining a gilt – progress route. JOHN GADD

Use your hands to feel the underline from front to back: it should feel soft and silky, and if any areas are rough take a closer look at the teats. Teats may have been permanently damaged – for example, rubbed off on rough floors – or are 'blind', where no orifice is present to let out the milk. Pig teats normally have two orifices (this varies) leading from two independent milk-producing glands. The teat may be inverted (inside out, rather like a sock), a condition that will make it difficult, if not impossible, for piglets to suckle. These teats are often short and broad, something like a button. Many partially inverted teats pop out once piglets start to suckle, but this is not always the case, so take care to detect this deformity. Remember, most piglets that die after birth, die from malnutrition: their own personal teat will either provide for life or starve them and result in their death.

Ideally, teats should be long enough for a tight grip during suckling, enabling even the smallest piglet to hang on and feed well in the few seconds that milk flows, and for them to survive, grow and thrive. It is potentially functional teats that we should be counting when selecting gilts, and this also applies to boars if they are to be used for breeding daughters and sons. If using artificial insemination, check out the boars. A BPA-type classification report will include all aspects of conformation, including teat details. These are available, so request them before using such boars for breeding replacements.

Gilts

In gilts, next examine the vulva and check that they have an anus. The vulva should not be of an abnormal shape or point upwards. If it is, take a closer look and use your fingers to examine the vulva and vagina, including the clitoris which can be oversized in abnormal females. It could be a hermaphrodite and therefore sterile. Time and money can

Blind anus in the male piglet.

be lost if hermaphrodites are selected for breeding. They often score well on carcase and growth characteristics due to the influence of male hormones, so performance test data should not be solely relied upon.

Blind Anus

A blind anus in gilts is a relatively common congenital fault which may also be genetic in origin. The actual cause is unknown and it occurs in both sexes. Surgical treatment in males is possible but rarely practicable, and most males will die if not culled humanely. At least half of the females survive because they dung through the vagina. These gilts are not equipped for breeding and should be sent off as normal slaughter pigs.

Hernias

Avoid selecting both males and females with evidence of a hernia – umbilical or scrotal – and reject these for breeding, as it may be a genetic weakness.

Additional Points when Selecting Boars

Check the testicles for evenness: there is some evidence that variation in testicle size is linked with reduced fertility. They will rarely be of identical size, but do feel them for any abnormal swelling. The penis and sheath should also be felt and examined. Investigate any lumps, and check the penis length if possible: some very lean young boars have short penises, making correct mating difficult. Up to 10 per cent of young replacement boars may not be fertile or may fail to mate; however, good and careful selection should reduce this level considerably.

Parasites, Skin and Bloom

Always check young boars and gilts for internal and external parasites (worms, lice and mange) prior to their entry into the breeding herd. Protect replacements against parasites using a programme devised together with your vet, and include an appropriate vaccination policy.

Replacement animals should have a smooth, silky coat and a shiny bloom, which indicates good health and the absence of parasites. Skin rashes and flabby muscles would warrant further investigation.

Fecundity

At its simplest, this term stands for the ability of a sow or gilt both to produce piglets and to rear them. It is also used to express the potential ability of a boar to pass this characteristic on to his daughters. Pedigree breeders must provide litter details to the BPA to notify for pedigree registration, and most breeding companies have achieved considerable success in improving fecundity by selecting 'hyperprolific' sows from very large populations. Even though it has a low heritability value, it is unwise to ignore fecundity.

Constitution and Temperament

Replacement breeding stock must have a constitution that will stand up to the conditions on the breeding unit. This will depend to a major degree on the breed chosen; for instance, outdoor pigs need to have a constitution that will ensure they continue to perform under harsh climatic conditions. Equally, temperament should be considered: for example, nervous animals will have great difficulty in fitting in to any unit, whether intensive or extensive in nature, so nervous or shy animals are best avoided.

CHOOSING THE GILT REPLACEMENT SYSTEM FOR YOUR HERD

The main options for commercial hybrid herds are:

- Purchased hybrid (cross-bred) gilts
- Purchased pure-bred grandparent gilts (or GGP)

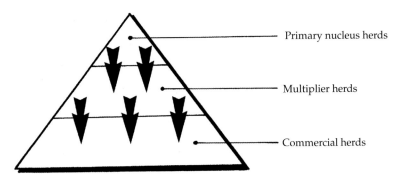

Primary nucleus herds

Multiplier herds

Commercial herds

The breeding pyramid.

- Home-bred grandparent gilts using AI
- 'Basic' criss-cross
- 'Improved' criss-cross
- Home-bred grandparent gilts and commercial boars

These six systems are examples of the methods of replacement adopted by UK commercial breeding herds with crossbred or hybrid sows. There are only two real options for most small- to medium-sized herds, and these are purchasing hybrid gilts, or improved criss-cross breeding. The former demands an open-herd policy, whilst the latter offers the possibility of a reasonably closed herd if artificial insemination is used extensively. Larger herds can maintain GGP and GP sow groups and use AI to maintain a completely closed herd status.

Pedigree Breeders or Rare Breed Herds

The problem that a small pedigree breeder has is similar to that of the rare breed enthusiast, namely of maintaining sufficient female and male lines and avoiding inbreeding. Popular breeds are not difficult to manage, but the less popular breeds pose a problem. It is a vicious circle, and only through regular importation of fresh blood lines can any progress be made and inbreeding avoided. This may pose serious health problems if stock have to be purchased from several sources.

Commercial Breeding Company Multipliers

These are normally independent farmers who contract either to multiply pure breeds for cross-breeding and/or to multiply the

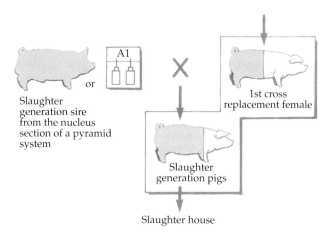

System 1 – Purchased hybrid gilts. MLC

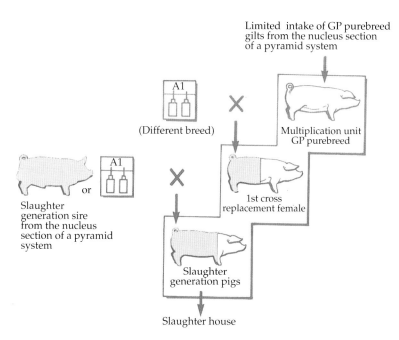

System 2 – Purchased pure-bred grandparent (GP) gilts. MLC

Fl hybrid gilts sold to commercial producers. These herds, although financially independent of the breeding company, must operate within strict breeding policy guidelines set down by that company.

BUYING AND SELLING WEANER PIGS

There are a number of pig marketing groups set up specifically to market the slaughter pig. They may also organize the sale and purchase of weaner pigs for their members. Weaner pigs can be sold directly at weaning, as early as four weeks of age, although this is a risky enterprise and the breeder must have a guaranteed outlet. Outdoor units will frequently sell their weaners directly from the field at weaning, and it is important that this is based on sound production contracts. It is really essential to tie up a firm contract with finishing herds for weaned piglets.

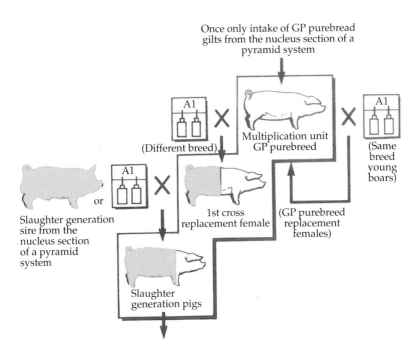

System 3 – Home-bred grandparent (GP) gilts. MLC

Pig marketing organizations – such as Thames Valley Cambac – also operate weaner sale and purchasing schemes. Typical prices are recorded in the weekly farming press or the BPEX web site. Selling weaners can be a problem when the market is oversupplied, and schemes can offer a contract price structure designed to even out the financial fluctuations. The purchaser should ensure that the health status of their source herds is good, and should set up an appropriate medication and introductory management policy in collaboration with their veterinary surgeon.

Some purchasers of weaner pigs operate the 'all-in, all-out' approach for batches of pigs, where a whole finishing house is depopulated between batches in order to reduce the transmission of disease. Weaner pigs are usually either purchased immediately at weaning from around 7kg, or reared on, often on a different site, until they are 30 to 35kg, when they are then either sold or transferred to finishing units.

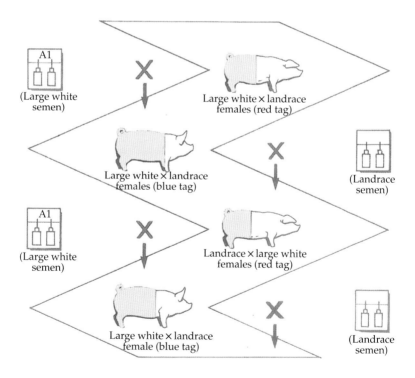

Systems 4 and 5 – Criss-cross method (basic and improved systems). MLC

Those starting with pigs for the first time can download the government pdf publication 'Guide for Pig Keepers': www.gov.uk/government/publications/a-guide-for-pig-keepers. This covers aspects such as the current procedures for registering the holding, identification of pigs, registration and on-farm records for pigs.

Whether you keep one pig as a pet or you run a commercial herd, you need to be registered with the Department for Environment, Food and Rural Affairs (Defra), and must observe the following legal structure:

- You must pre-notify all movement of pigs from your holding
- All pigs going to slaughter must be identified with their herd mark
- Owners of a pet pig must not move it other than to another holding – or walk it – without obtaining a walking licence from their AHVLA Regional Office. The route will need to

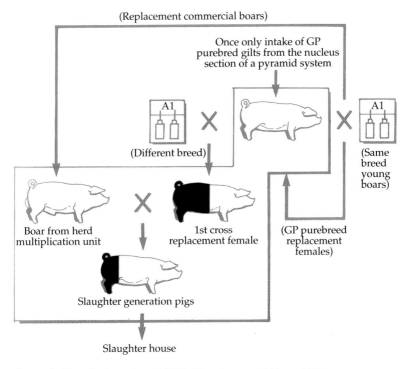

System 6 – Home-bred grandparent (GP) gilts and commercial boars. MLC be pre-approved, and a licence must be carried by the keeper during the walk. (Source: 'A guide for pig keepers' DEFRA August,/2013.)

Laws, rules and regulations can change and will also vary in different countries, and it is the pig keeper's responsibility to be apprised and up to date. To view the eAML2 electronic movement licence details go to the following web sites: www.britishpigs.org. uk/eaml2_intro.htm and www.countrywidefarmers.co.uk/pws/ pdf/how_to_guides/How_to_Smallholder_choose_and_keep_ pigs.pdf.

Breeds at Risk Register

DEFRA in partnership with the devolved administrations in Northern Ireland, Scotland and Wales is setting up a register of farms with rare breeds. In the event of an outbreak of foot of mouth disease this register will be used by local government vets to check which herds may be eligible for possible vaccination. The register will cover the whole of the United Kingdom.

BPA's investments in computer technology mean that they can transfer all the required information directly from their pedigree database to the DEFRA register. BPA members do *not* have to register directly with DEFRA or with the Rare Breeds Survival Trust.

The breeds which are considered 'at risk' at present are the Berkshire, British Saddleback, Gloucestershire Old Spot, Large Black, Middle White, Oxford Sandy and Black, Tamworth and Welsh. *See also* Further Information for details of the government websites. Also see: archive.defra.gov.uk/foodfarm/farmanimal/diseases/atoz/ fmd/about/riskreg.htm and www.accidentalsmallholder.net/forum/ index.php?topic=30102.0.

3

The Nutritional Needs of the Pig

All animals aim to achieve a genetically predetermined mature body-weight. In growing pigs for slaughter, maturity is best defined as the point when the growth of muscle reaches its maximum, and uneconomical fat begins to be laid down in rapidly increasing amounts. The pig's ability to reach this point is influenced by its supply of nutrients, its health status, and the social, structural and climatic environment in which it lives. Pig breeders who have selected pigs for ever-increasing growth rates have also probably bred an animal of greater mature size. In order to understand the reasons why pigs of different ages need to be fed diets with certain levels of nutrients, it is worth examining the make-up of a pig at birth and then at 50kg.

Pigs grow extremely quickly and by three weeks of age the typical piglet will already contain 12 to 15 per cent body fat. The modern weaned piglet probably has more fat as a percentage of its body at four weeks of age than it will have as a percentage of its carcase at 100kg live weight. Protein and water with very small amounts of fat make up the lean (muscle). Sow's milk provides the piglet with high levels of fat and protein which are necessary for it to grow and develop.

Pig rations must aim to provide the growing animal with all the nutrients it requires at each stage of its development. In breeding adults, diet requirement will vary according to where the female is in her reproductive and rearing cycle. In the boar it will depend on how hard he is working. The diagram illustrates the change in diet necessary to make optimum use of the pig's developing ability to digest nutrients.

THE PIG'S DIGESTIVE SYSTEM

The pig has a digestive system which appears similar in outline to that of the human. Like the human, the pig has the ability to eat

Live weight (kg)	Protein (kg)	Fat (kg)	Mineral/Water	
			Ash (kg)	(kg)
1.25	0.14	0.013	0.04	1.01
	(11%)	(1%)	(4%)	(81%)
50.00	7.5	11.0	1.50	30.00
	(15%)	(22%)	(3%)	(60%)

The baby pig will also contain about 2.5 per cent glycogen (blood sugar) at birth.

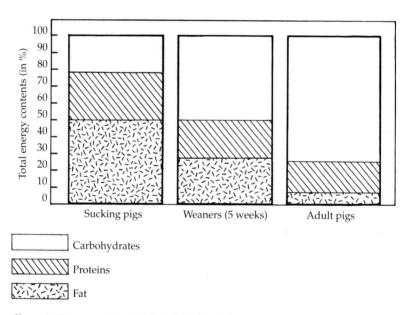

Carbohydrates

Proteins

Fat

Change in the composition of the feed of pigs in relation to age. AUMAITRE

a wide range of foods. However, this omnivorous feeding ability extends well beyond the human range, and pigs can utilize bulky higher fibre diets.

The lining of the small intestine is a highly sophisticated aid to food digestion and absorption, with large numbers of small finger-like projections called villi. In pigs the villi are shorter in length than in other farm animals and can suffer rapid damage. The large intestines in young and immature animals are chiefly involved with the absorption of water into the body, having a small role in absorbing

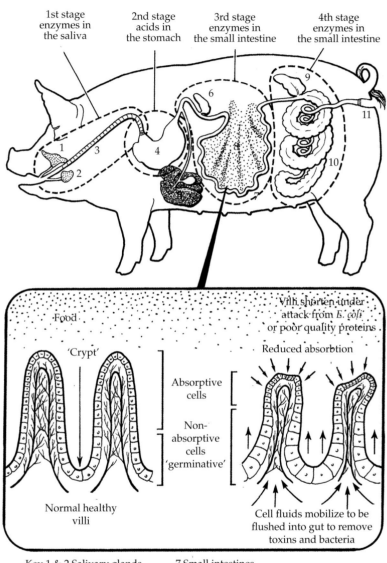

1st stage enzymes in the saliva

2nd stage acids in the stomach

3rd stage enzymes in the small intestine

4th stage enzymes in the small intestine

Food

Villi shorten under attack from *E. coli* or poor quality proteins

'Crypt'

Reduced absorbtion

Absorptive cells

Non-absorptive cells 'germinative'

Normal healthy villi

Cell fluids mobilize to be flushed into gut to remove toxins and bacteria

Key 1 & 2 Salivary glands
3 Oesophagus
4 Stomach
5 Liver and Gall bladder
6 Pancreas

7 Small intestines
8 Caul (Omentum)
9 Calcum
10 Large intestine
11 Rectum and anus

Digestion in the pig.

certain vitamins produced by the gut micro-organisms. The large intestines operate in a more alkaline environment and secrete mucus to lubricate undigested food. During scours (diarrhoea), fluids containing electrolytes (body salts) are released to dilute the irritating factors, and this rapidly leads to dehydration.

In adult pigs the bacteria in the large intestine and caecum are similar to those found in the rumen of sheep or cattle and the caecum of horses. These bacteria break down soluble fibre and provide energy, which is absorbed in the form of 'volatile fatty acids'; these are similar in nature to vinegar (acetic acid). Unfortunately, pigs cannot digest the considerable quantities of these helpful microbes when these die and gain protein from them, as is the case in ruminants. They are invariably lost in the dung, and it is not normal for the pig to eat its own faeces.

Nonetheless, in adult pigs, grazing young grass and even eating specially conserved bulk fodder in the form of highly digestible low-fibre silage can be a useful source of economical food energy. Fodder beet can also be fed to pigs, and mature sows have been known to consume up to 30kg of wet material in a day. This equates with around 5kg of barley meal (an excessive intake), which needs to be reduced and balanced with a protein concentrate.

The microbes that live in the small and large intestines have tremendous influence on the effectiveness of digestion. Probiotic feed additives, based on bacteria such as the lactobacillus found in yoghurt, are being used increasingly to maintain a healthy microbe intestine population and to aid efficient digestion in young pigs. Acidified milk replacers are also useful in maintaining a healthy gut environment.

FEEDING THE PIG

Diet Energy

We normally consider fats, sugars, other carbohydrates and some protein to be the major sources of energy. The energy content of feed is measured in units called joules, which can be related to the more widely known unit of heat called the calorie (1 calorie = 4.184 joules). We normally measure energy as mega-joules (MJ). More than 70 per cent of the diet cost is energy, and around 80 per cent of all costs are for feed in growing pigs. There are three basic ways of describing energy levels in pig nutrition: digestible energy (DE), metabolizable energy (ME), and net energy (NE).

Approximate Conversion Factors for Energy Density

Feed	DE MJ/kg	ME MJ/kg	NE MJ/kg
Creep	16.60	15.85	12.00
Grower/finisher	14.20	13.60	10.30
Home mix finisher	12.92	12.32	9.33
Sow/breeding	12.73	12.15	9.20

The values in the table are examples only, and there is no fixed conversion factor between each approach. The DE system remains the easiest method to use when describing the energy density of feeds on farm. Nutritionists producing compound feeds or concentrate mixes for use on farm also use an NE system when computing the quantities of each feed component (for example wheat, soya) to include in the mix. NE takes into account the different feed components and the diet nutrients protein, fat, starch, fibre and also sugars. These can also be related to the age, weight and growth rate of the pig. NE describes feed energy using the same 'currency' as the animal's needs. The contribution of dietary nutrients to energy supply in growing pigs is illustrated below:

Adult pigs will make reasonably efficient use of dietary fibre and therefore they will have a slightly higher NE feed value for diets containing more digestible fibre. The NE system allows for this difference between growing and adult pigs.

The example given in the table above indicates the negative effect that dietary fibre has on the NE achieved in growing pigs. It also illustrates that fat provides twice the energy derived from starch, and two and a half times that of protein on a weight-for-weight basis.

With reference to the table above, sugars can also be included in the nutrient list, with typical values: DE 16.1, ME 15.9, and NE 11.5 per kg of sugar. Sugar would have an ME to NE utilization of about 72 per cent.

Contribution of Nutrients to Energy Supply in Growing Pigs as a % of Starch

Nutrient	Starch	Fat	Crude protein	Dietary fibre
Gross energy	100	221	129	106
DE	100	174	123	3
ME	100	177	109	3
NE	100	195	80	−6

Source: Noble, J., *Recent Developments in Net Energy Research for Pigs*, ASAS 2008.

Efficiency of ME Utilization for the Various Nutrients

Crude protein	58%
Crude fat	90%
Starch	82%
Dietary fibre	58%

Source: Noble, J., *Recent Developments in Net Energy Research for Pigs*, ASAS 2008.

The energy measurements GE, DE, ME and NE are taken at different stages of digestion and metabolism in the body of the pig. The procedure for measuring food energy involves testing it in a special calorimeter that measures the gross energy (GE). When the energy is digested we lose some of this energy in the faeces (dung). The dung can also be tested in the same way, and can tell us how much was not digested and give the DE value. Digestibility is typically about 82 per cent for a compound diet.

It gets a little more complicated with ME. The losses between DE and ME are contained in the urine and gaseous escapes in the form of methane. Sophisticated equipment is necessary to collect the urine and gas to allow them to be measured. We usually lose between 3 and 6 per cent of the feed energy between the DE and ME values. The body uses the metabolizable energy for growth, exercise, bodily functions and maintenance requirements. The metabolic processes then

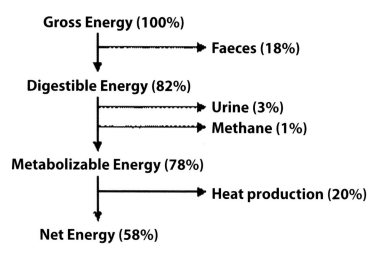

An example of how energy is utilized in the pig from a typical compound feed.

generate heat, which is then lost from the body. This accounts for a loss of about 20 to 25 per cent of the energy measured as ME in a feed mixture. This loss difference is then used to determine NE. Therefore, NE is about three-quarters of the ME value for a compound diet.

To summarize: if we take GE as 100 per cent, DE will be around 82 per cent, ME will be 78 per cent and NE about 58 per cent of GE, respectively. The NE values of individual feed ingredients and the main nutrients as listed above are far more varied. This illustrates why the NE approach offers far more precision in describing the 'true' energy value of a diet to a pig of a particular age at a specified weight and growth rate.

Practical Application

The DE system is usually the method used and referred to on farm. Compound feed manufacturers and nutritionists will use an NE system to refine the precision of their diet formulation. NE systems are now part of the armoury that allows the nutritionist to tailor the diet to the pigs of a specific genetic make-up, age and weight. There is an impelling case for, and a trend towards, formulating specific diets for individual farm situations.

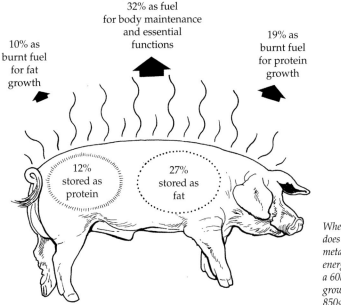

32% as fuel for body maintenance and essential functions

10% as burnt fuel for fat growth

19% as burnt fuel for protein growth

12% stored as protein

27% stored as fat

Where does the metabolizable energy go in a 60kg pig growing at 850g per day?

Where does the energy go to in a typical pig? This depends on many factors, including the amount of lean and fat the pig grows, and if it lives in a cold environment, in which it must keep itself warm with food energy. The diagram illustrates where the energy goes to in a pig during the latter part of the finishing period beyond 50kg live weight. The diagram also shows that 40 per cent of the feed energy is used for the maintenance of essential body functions before any of it is available for work and growth – this is usually 35 to 40 per cent of the energy intake from a typical compound feed.

Sources of Energy

Fats and Oils

Fats and oils contain approximately twice the energy content of proteins and carbohydrates, and they also usually generate less heat production. This is particularly useful when providing lactating sows with high energy intakes during hot weather in outdoor breeding pigs in the UK and in countries with hot climates.

Fats and oils are added to diets in order to increase the energy content of the final product. They may be mixed into or sprayed on to the pelleted feed. Fats contain varying levels of saturated and polyunsaturated fats. Vitamin E levels must be adjusted upwards when more fats and especially where polyunsaturated fatty acids are used, otherwise an increase in sudden death through heart failure will occur in growing and finishing pigs.

Fat is often given on a feed analysis sheet as the percentage ether extract – typically 3 to 5 per cent. Fats vary considerably in their digestibility, depending on quality (range: 20 to 80 per cent) – for example, milk fat is highly digestible.

Starch and Sugars

Starch makes up around 70 per cent of the diet by dry weight, and is usually around 95 per cent digestible, although if mixed with fibre, digestibility will fall considerably. Optimum grinding helps the digestive juices to get at the starch to digest it.

Fibre

It is important to note that the level of fibre affects digestibility. Very young pigs require very low levels of fibre, whilst sows are happy with 6 per cent and above. As a general rule, growing pigs like around 4 per cent. For every 1 per cent that fibre exceeds the pig's maximum, the digestibility of feed energy falls by about 4 per cent. Protein digestion will be affected in a similar way.

The name fibre refers not to a single substance but to a range of substances related to cellulose (plant cell walls), gums (pectin) and in mature plants, woody tissue known as lignin. All of these are indigestible to the enzymes in the pig's digestive system, but some are soluble and soak up water, such as pectins, hemicelluloses and oligosaccharides. These can be more easily fermented by gut microorganisms to release energy in the caecum and large intestine.

There is considerable evidence to indicate that in pregnant sows increased intakes of fibrous materials, such as straw, leads to a more contented animal. This does make sense, because the gut capacity (dry matter appetite) of a pregnant sow is around 4.5kg of dry feed each day. We normally only need to feed 2 to 3kg at the most, and this leaves around 2.5kg of unfilled space. It is, however, important to remember that the sow needs a proportion of her diet in a concentrated form, and the high-fibre part of the diet should be seen as a top-up ingredient. The aim should be to ensure the sow has adequate protein provision in the diet before any of the feed gets into the intestine.

Digestible fibre, which is broken down by the bacteria and fermented in the large intestine, can provide very economical energy to the sow in the form of volatile fatty acids (acetate, propionate and butyrate). Breeding boars can be fed in a similar fashion.

It is uneconomical to feed growing pigs on high-fibre diets, so do take great care on this important point.

Grinding and Meal Texture

Pigs need their feed ground fairly finely. Digestibility will be affected in a similar fashion to fibre levels if coarse or only broken grains are fed. If home milling and mixing, always take expert advice on the degree of grinding necessary with various raw materials.

Making up Rations Based on Energy

If we take some simple common ingredients we could make up a home-mix low-density diet, as indicated in the table. We could increase the energy level of this simple diet by replacing some of the barley with wheat, or, as is often the case with modern high-density diets, by adding high-energy fats and oils. The protein, mineral

Ingredients for a Home-Mix Low-Density Diet

Barley – DE MJ/kg = 13.1 – use 75%	=9.83
Wheat – DE MJ/kg = 13.7 – use 10%	=1.37
White fish meal – DE MJ/kg = 13.0 – use 12%	=1.56
Minerals/vitamins – use 3%	
Total energy in 1kg of the diet	=12.76 MJ/DE

and cost elements must also be considered, but the table does illustrate the relatively simple calculations involved with the MJ/DE/kg approach. It is not a legal requirement for UK feed manufacturers to declare the energy content of any diet sold by them; however, most compounders will provide this information in outline upon request.

European pig-feed compounders have tended to produce high-energy diets. When feed prices were relatively low this is probably correct, but with an increase in feed ingredient costs there is a financial argument in favour of producing lower energy density diets. Energy costs money, and we must aim to use it as effectively as possible. This will partly explain why we may see changes in the concentration of energy density values over time. It is important to remember that we are aiming to get the optimum amount of protein, energy, minerals and vital elements into the pig. Lower density diets have to be fed at higher daily feed intake levels than high density diets, and it is important to remember this when comparing feeding scales.

Even if a pig is not growing, it has a maintenance requirement for energy, which must be satisfied before growth of any form can take place. This usually accounts for about 35 to 40 per cent of the feed energy. It also illustrates the possibility of reducing the amount of energy stored in body fat, and increasing the amount available for maximum protein growth. Furthermore, if pigs are kept below their lower critical temperature (LCT) they will use some of the energy to keep warm; this would otherwise be used to drive the laying down and storage of energy as body protein or fat. To understand this further we need to consider the next major nutrient: protein.

Protein

When we buy a pig diet we tend to look at the protein level, which is given as a crude protein percentage of the diet on the feed bag or bulk delivery ticket. Pig farmers and feed company representatives will frequently refer to the crude protein level of their various pig diets. For example:

High density creep – 21 to 24%
Grower or weaner – 21 to 22%
Finisher – 18 to 19%
Gestating sow and boar – 12 to 14%
Lactating sow – 16 to 18%

However, these figures tell us very little about the actual quantity and quality of the protein available to the pig. First, protein digestibility will normally vary between 80 and 85 per cent. If we take two diets from two different feed manufacturers, with the same crude protein percentage on the delivery ticket, and feed it to a standard pig, a typical digestibility and level of utilization may be seen in the diagrams.

The feedstuffs compounder will usually disclose the lysine level as a percentage of the total diet. This is a very useful piece of information about the quality of the protein in the feed and will indicate if it is appropriate to use, as illustrated in the diagrams below. Diet X would probably contain around 1 per cent lysine compared to 1.4 per cent in Y. In this particular pig (specific weight, breed, age and growth rate) it is clear that the higher lysine diet is used more efficiently. This underlines the fact that although the protein percentage tells us about the concentration of protein, we must be given the lysine level to help define protein quality.

Excesses of other amino acids will also occur in protein-rich raw materials, such as soya bean meal. The animal has to dispose of those amino acids in excess by breaking them down (catabolism), and these will be excreted as expensive and potentially polluting nitrates in the urine. The 'optimum' higher lysine level in diet Y serves as a good indicator that there is a good balance of amino acids as compared to diet X. Excessively high lysine diets will also lead to expensive inefficiency. The potential effects of amino acid quality defined by the lysine levels are illustrated in the accompanying diagrams.

The available lysine level in the diet is useful for defining protein quality on farm. This is because lysine is the most limiting and the first and most essential amino acid not to be available at adequate levels for the pig to produce proteins in its tissues, digestive enzymes, blood, antibodies, milk protein and hormones. This will

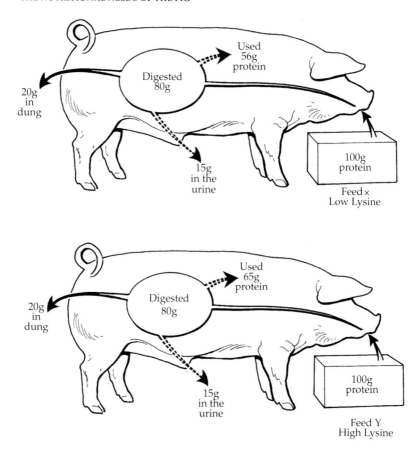

Protein quality as seen by how much of it is useful to the pig.

limit the quantity of these proteins that can be produced by the body, and is why it is referred to as the first limiting amino acid.

There are approximately twenty-two amino acids in pig protein, and the pig can produce about 60 per cent of them itself from the diet. There are ten that are all potentially 'limiting' or, better said, are what are termed as 'essential amino acids,' along with two that are 'half essential'. They are also essential for normal health and metabolic processes. 'Ideal' protein describes a diet amino acid profile that is theoretically exactly the same as that required for producing

Ideal Protein

	Piglet	Grower	Finisher
Lysine	100	100	100
Methionine + cystine	60	60	60
Threonine	65	67	68
Tryptophan	22	20	19
Valine	70	>65	>65
Isoluecine	53	53	53
Leucine	100	100	100
Histidine	32	32	32
Phenylalanine + tyrosine	95	95	95
Arginine	42	42	42

Note: Cystine and tyrosine can be described as 'half-essential' because they can be produced from their paired amino acid: for example, cystine can be made from its fellow sulphur-containing amino acid methionine.

pig protein. Lysine and the other essential amino acids, such as methionine, must be available in the diet and cannot be synthesized. The aim when formulating pig diets is to get as close as economically possible to the ideal amino acid profile. This is assisted by the modern availability of synthetic amino acids when these are added to the feed mixture during compounding and home mixing.

The table above shows the ideal protein profile example for growing pigs expressed relative to lysine, based on the digestibility percentage of lysine (SID): Ajinomoto-Eurolysine.com 2013.

As a general rule it can be said that the young pig needs more protein and higher lysine concentrations in its diet than older pigs. This makes sense because the young pig converts feed more efficiently. It follows that young growing piglets require more protein for each unit of energy compared to older and larger animals. Entire male animals also require higher lysine levels because they can grow more lean meat each day than gilts, and considerably more than castrates. Likewise, improved high performance pigs require higher lysine levels than the slower growing, early maturing and fatter unimproved breeds.

In practice, we should pay attention to the quality of the diet by insisting on details of the energy and available lysine levels and matching these to the type of pig we have to feed. The following are useful examples in feed formulation and as a guide when purchasing feed stuffs. (Insist on this information if it is not provided.) Lysine is frequently defined using the term 'digestible lysine'.

Nutrients per Kilogram of Fresh Feed

Live weight range (kg)	MJ/DE	Protein (g)	Lysine (g) (% of diet)
0–20	17.0	230	16.0 (1.6%)
20–40	15.0	200	13.0 (1.3%)
40–60	14.0	190	11.0 (1.1%)
60–80	13.0	170	9.5 (0.95%)
80–100	12.5	150	7.5 (0.75%)

A 10 to 20kg pig eating one kilogram of the 230g per kilogram diet will, of course, consume 230g of protein, and within that protein it consumes 16g of lysine. Using diets that are too low in lysine may well save on feed costs, but it will usually be a false economy, as the following table shows.

As pigs get heavier and older their requirement for lysine falls and their energy needs increase, and phase feeding three diets as shown in the diagram helps keep the lysine in step: the red line shows that this lysine requirement falls in relation to energy as the pig grows. Phase feeding offers an effective method of optimizing protein intake and growth.

Optimum growth depends on a specific energy/lysine balance, and this will need to be matched to your pigs. Entire male pigs respond to higher lysine than castrates, so do not waste excess lysine or, for that matter, excess protein on unimproved pigs. Also, do not over-feed lysine or protein to high performance pigs, because it will merely be converted into a very expensive component of liquid fertilizer in the urine and will add to the risk of environmental pollution.

Always take expert advice and feed the appropriate diets to your pigs and remember that feed accounts for 75 to 80 per cent

Comparison of Dietary Regime (5–90kg live weight)

	Diets with adequate ideal protein	Diets 10% deficient in lysine	Difference (poorer)
Feed conversion efficiency	2.25:1	2.43:1	8%
Live-weight gain/day (g)	660	605	8%
Lean tissue growth/day (g)	300	270	10%

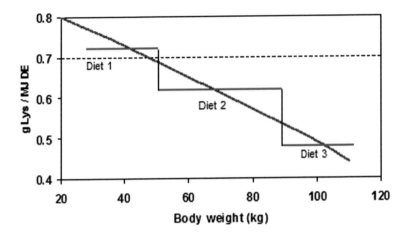

Optimum growth with phase feeding.

of total costs in growing and finishing pigs. If the feed conversion efficiency – FCE – (ratio) deteriorates by 8 per cent, this will cost around £6 per pig between 7kg (weaning) and 110kg live weight (2013 prices and the FCE is poorer by 0.2). The cost of adding extra amino acids, many of them synthetic and specially produced for animal feeds, will be far below this. Feed manufacturers and their expert nutritionists can now adjust the amino acid profile closer to the ideal protein described above, and although lysine level is a good guide, modern compound diets need no longer be compared simply using their lysine content. Ultimately, it is animal performance and economics that define feed and protein quality, along with their potential environmental impact.

Just like energy, the protein content, expressed as a percentage of the diet by weight, is assessed according to how cost effective and appropriate it is to the animal it is fed to. Today and in the future we must also consider the environmental impact of high crude protein diets as compared to a potentially less polluting reduction in the percentage of crude protein. Nutrient densities are not written in tablets of stone, and what may be correct at a particular point in time may not be in the future. Likewise, what may be the 'optimum' today in the EU may not provide the best diet economics for pigs in North or South America, or in Asia.

Water

This important nutrient is often forgotten or underestimated, and the minimum target should be a fresh supply of clean, uncontaminated drinking water in sufficient quantities to meet pig requirements. The penalties for failing to meet these requirements are very severe:

Reduced appetite and feed refusal
Dehydration
Salt poisoning
Stress and aggressive behaviour
Reduced growth rate and poorer feed conversion efficiency
Reduced sow milk yield and piglet starvation
Cystitis/nephritis infection in sows

Pigs should be given as much water as they want and they need to be able to drink it quickly. Actual consumption will probably vary by plus or minus 40 to 60 per cent, so allow for the estimated upper limits. Pigs can consume additional water even when fed liquid feed up to a very soupy 3.5:1 ratio of water to meal. The following consumption levels are an upper limit guide for calculating water supply safety levels, or emergency tanker supply requirements for outdoor herds.

Pig type and weight	Litres per day	Minutes taken to drink 1 litre
Piglets to 15kg	2	4
15–40kg	3	2
40–60kg	6	1.25
60kg plus	7–8.5	1
Dry sow	8–15	40 sec
Suckling sow	20–40	down to 20 sec

The daily water requirement for a pig is approximately 10 per cent of its bodyweight, as indicated above. These values are for estimating requirements only, and in normal weather conditions less consumption might be expected. The time taken to drink one litre is useful in estimating drinker flow rates, which need to exceed 250 millilitres per minute for piglets just after weaning, and at least one litre per minute for gestating sows. According to researchers in the USA, some sows drink at a rate of two litres per minute, especially during lactation. Test your drinker flow rates right away and investigate potential improvements.

Water is not much use when frozen.

Sows breaking through ice to drink.

Tractor-drawn water tankers (bowsers) are essential to provide outdoor pigs with water in sub-zero weather. They are equally important to create muddy wallows during very hot, sunny weather.

Cube drinker in a straw-based weaner pen.

Drinking from a bite drinker on a Turbomat round feeder.

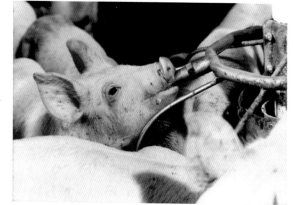

Temporary piglet feeders in the covered runs of Trobridge weaner bungalows with 'piglet porridge' to encourage feed/ fluid intake. This also illustrates a suspended 'toy' designed to enrich the piglet's environment.

There are many types of drinker, ranging from nipple drinkers, bite drinkers and nose-operated drinkers through to water bowls of various shapes and sizes. Open troughs will undoubtedly speed up intake, but the water must be as clean and fresh as anything a human would wish to consume. Cube drinkers are an excellent method of ensuring that piglets achieve their full water and feed intake immediately after weaning. But do not forget to change the water at least twice a day, and soak the drinkers in disinfectant between pig batches. Turkey drinkers are an excellent alternative for weaners, and can be directly connected to the water supply.

We can state quite confidently that the number of drinkers is less important than flow rate. One drinker per ten pigs is recommended. Drinker height is important, and the 45-degree type is probably more comfortable for the pig to get the water. The Danish National Committee for Pig Breeding and Production Annual Report for 1987 gave the following recommendations for nipple drinker heights:

Pig Weight Range (kg)	Nipple 90° (cm)	Nipple 45° (cm)
Pre-weaning piglet	10	15
5–15	25–35	30–45
5–20	25–40	30–50
7–15	30–35	35–45
7–25	30–45	35–55
15–30	35–45	45–55
15–50	35–55	45–65
20–50	40–55	50–65
25–50	45–55	55–65
25–100	45–65	55–75
50–100	55–65	65–75
Sows and boars	70–80	80–90

If more than one drinker is used, always make sure that they are set far enough apart, ideally the length of a pig. The Turbomat round feeder has a number of drinkers sited above the trough, and these make water available at all times during feeding. The 'single space' or 'mix-at-the-trough' feeders provide a drinker so that the pig can mix water with its feed; a similar arrangement is found in farrowing house feed troughs.

Warming water to 10–15°C in winter has been found beneficial for weaned piglets in Germany; this apparently avoids shocking the piglet's system. Soda water (water saturated with carbon dioxide) has been provided in the USA during heat stress periods; it is claimed that appetites are maintained in extreme environmental conditions.

Additional water should be provided for weaner pigs in easily available containers, such as cube drinkers or turkey drinkers as an extra initial supply. Weaner pigs are known to become dehydrated and to stop feeding for long periods after weaning, which is extremely wasteful and potentially life-threatening. Although food is an important element, sufficient water intake is essential for good post-weaning growth.

Various flavour-based products are available to mix with the water in a cube drinker or to a header tank to encourage piglets to drink, and it is claimed that this can help bring the piglet's feed intake back to normal within three to four days post weaning. It is also claimed to be especially effective if they have consumed some of this prior to weaning. There are also products containing an electrolyte solution, which can be put into the water in cube drinkers at weaning. Electrolytes help to combat dehydration and improve gut health.

Water is an ideal method of medicating pigs, and there are a number of water-medicating devices on the market that can be attached to the water-supply pipe to the pen. However, water-delivered antibiotics should never become a routine after weaning, and must always be carried out under the supervision of a veterinarian and with a veterinary prescription.

Minerals in Pig Diets

About 75 per cent of the mineral content of a pig is made up of calcium and phosphorus, whilst the remainder is almost all potassium and sodium with some magnesium, chlorine and sulphur. These are the major mineral elements in pig nutrition and they are usually measured as a percentage of the diet. Trace elements include iron, copper, cobalt, iodine, manganese, zinc, selenium, molybdenum and chromium; these are measured in parts per million or milligrams per kilogram of the diet.

These trace elements are just as important as the major elements, and a deficiency can cause serious problems. For example, a deficiency of iron will cause anaemia (haemoglobin < 80 to 100g/litre of blood) in a young piglet, but it also has an influence on its growth potential and its immune system both before and after weaning. The iron concentration in piglets at birth is 20–30ppm: of this concentration in the piglet, 40 per cent is associated with blood, 1.6 per cent in the spleen, 15 per cent in the liver, and the remaining 44 per cent is found in body tissues. Following the neonatal period, around 80 per cent of the iron in the pig is associated with haemoglobin (Hb).

Controlling feed phosphorus excretion in pig dung and slurry is also an important issue. This is achieved by lowering its inclusion and improving its availability using phytase additives.

Minerals have many functions in the body and these include:

Structural (for example, bones)
Enzyme activators
Cellular function and metabolism

For example, calcium is used for the skeleton and teeth, nerve impulses, muscle contraction (necessary with the hormone oxytocin), and blood clotting. Calcium must not exceed a ratio of three parts to one part phosphorus; this is extremely important if vitamin D levels are low.

Sodium and salt levels are also critical in pigs. They will die rapidly from salt poisoning, caused by either insufficient water or excess salt. Always pay particular attention to the recommended salt levels, especially if feeding whey-type feeds or other potentially high salt ingredients.

If diets are well designed and monitoring is good, then both the major and trace mineral levels should be close to feeding recommendations. It is interesting to note that selenium is now frequently listed with the vitamins despite it being a mineral required at trace element levels. The nutritional health effects and importance of Vitamin E and selenium have long been linked, and there is considerable evidence supporting the notion that pigs frequently suffer from a deficiency of one or both of these vital substances. Selenium inclusion must be in a suitable form (for example, Se yeast such as Selplex), and excess provision is extremely toxic.

Vitamins

Like many human foods, pig diets now contain adequate levels of vitamins, but circumstances can occur that lead to deficiencies. The development of vitamins prepared industrially and some with a totally synthetic form and very stable nature has ensured that few reactions can occur during feed storage. Vitamins are normally added at adequate levels.

Particular care is taken with the levels of vitamin D and vitamin A. An excess supply of vitamin D is linked to the availability of calcium and phosphorus in the body, and an excess of vitamin A may cause problems with the muscle-protecting role of vitamin E. Vitamin E and selenium are also considered to be important in protecting the pig when newly harvested grain is included in the feed mix.

This will be for about four to eight weeks after harvest. It is now known that enzymes in the 'ripening' grain produce 'free radicals' that are extremely damaging to the pig's cells. Avoiding fresh grain for eight weeks after harvesting is also a sensible precaution.

Feed Additives and Performance Enhancers

Pig feeds now contain a number of additives in addition to mineral and vitamin supplements. These perform a wide range of very important nutritional and health-related tasks. They include the following:

- Antimicrobial agents (antibiotics on prescription – health and growth)
- Probiotics and prebiotics (stabilize and maintain digestion)
- Enzymes and proteases (for digestion and growth)
- Mycotoxin binders and antioxidants (for example Mycosorb A+)
- Oral vaccines (for general health)
- Anthelmintics (for health, in particular for the control of worms)
- Flavouring, colouring and texturing agents (appetite/waste)
- Acidifying agents and essential oils (digestion and health)
- Chelating agents for minerals (for the easier digestion of minerals)
- Preservatives, antifungal and antiprotozoal agents (health)
- Emulsifying agents for liquid diets (fat for baby pigs)
- Phytase, an enzyme that increases the availability of phosphorus
- Phytogenic feed additives (phytobiotics, derived from plants)

Additives are primarily used to improve and maintain animal health and performance. Carcase modifiers are allowed in some countries, but these are banned in the EU and many other countries. Export/import restrictions often apply against countries that allow their use, and there is considerable consumer concern. Unfortunately, confusion remains amongst consumers relating to that fact that they have been banned for decades within the EU.

Whilst probiotics are live cultures of beneficial organisms, prebiotics are food substances such as oligosaccharides that selectively stimulate the growth of favourable species of bacteria in the gut (for example Alltech ActigenTM). They are often more effective where there is an underlying problem, and this could well be due to the fact that where gut conditions are already improved the effect is no longer as significant. The more advanced prebiotics are very effective and can produce significant economic returns on the cost of their inclusion, because most normal health herds have underlying digestion problems.

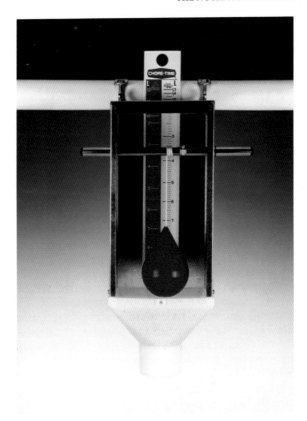

Calibrating a volumetric feed dispenser. An auger located in the white tube delivers feed to the dispenser. The feed is held by the plastic stopper attached to a cable, and this is wound up to allow simultaneous feed release down a delivery pipe into the trough for an individual sow. The amount of feed is set using a volume adjustment ruler. It is essential to check the weight/density of the feed at regular intervals. This calibration applies whether we are feeding using a feed scoop, a bucket, or volume-based feed dispensers.

Probiotics certainly appear to have a place in aiding recovery from a digestive disorder. An example of a probiotic is 'natural' live yoghurt, and this can be useful in helping restore and maintain gut health in piglets.

There are strict controls for the use of antimicrobials in animal feeds, and these are subject to use as prescription-only medicines. Antibiotic growth promoters were banned from use in 2006 in all EU countries.

Bulk feed storage silos must be cleaned regularly and kept in good condition to avoid mouldy feed. Mould and fungal (mycotoxins) contamination of feed will have severe pig health and performance consequences (mycotoxicosis).

Feed Ingredients and Anti-Nutritional Factors

Feed ingredients in pig feeds are mostly of plant origin, or meat and fish by-products. The most important ingredients are cereals and their by-products, oil seeds, pulses and some root crops and related by-products. However, it is not often understood that many of these contain anti-nutritional factors that can lower performance, such as the digestive enzyme trypsin inhibitor in soya bean and raw potatoes. Over millions of years plants have attempted to make themselves less attractive to the browsing and grazing animal, so it is important to include no more than the recommended amounts of various ingredients in specific diets.

Other industrial by-products include C-starch and even potato protein. Waste, or better said, by-products or co-products from breweries, distilleries, bakeries, sugar refiners and other industrial processes, such as bioethanol fuel manufacture, also provide useful and potentially cost-effective feed ingredients.

Always take impartial nutritional advice when planning the use of feedstuffs.

Milk and Dairy By-Products

These do not normally include large quantities of whole milk, but the by-products of cream, yoghurt, butter and cheese manufacture. Skimmed milk is increasingly consumed by humans and it also makes a very useful, well balanced ingredient in pig feed when available. Whey is the by-product of cheese manufacture and is an excellent energy source, also containing very high quality protein, albeit at low levels, and it will substitute some of the feed cereal ingredients. Registration with Defra is required – *see* below.

IMPORTANT FEED ADVICE FROM DEFRA (04/2013)

Following the outbreak of Foot and Mouth disease in 2001, the first case of which was found to be at a farm where unprocessed waste food was being fed to pigs, the Government carried out a review of the practice of swill feeding. The outbreak and subsequent review led to legislation banning the feeding of catering waste to any farmed animals or any other ruminant animal, pig or poultry. This is now reflected in EU-wide legislation. It is illegal to feed any pig any catering waste (including used cooking oil) from restaurants, kitchens (both household and central), and other catering facilities even if those establishments cater solely for vegetarians. Current legislation also imposes strict controls banning the feeding of other materials of animal origin or products containing them to farmed animals. There are, however, a small number of exceptions to this, and the following materials may be fed to pigs:

- Liquid milk or colostrum may be fed to pigs kept on the same holding as that on which the milk or colostrum originated
- Former foodstuffs other than catering waste food from kitchens etc. (*see* above) containing rennet, melted fat, milk or eggs but where these materials are not the main ingredient
- Fishmeal, (animal derived) di- or tri-calcium phosphate, or blood products if suitably processed (*see* TSE Regulations internet link below); and
- Milk, milk products and white water when suitably treated

Please note that anyone obtaining waste milk, milk products or white water to feed to their pigs would need to register with Defra for this purpose, although in the case of milk products, this would only be necessary it they contained more than 80 per cent milk. Details on how to register are available from either the Defra helpline (08459 33 55 77) or the internet archive.defra.gov.uk/foodfarm/farmanimal/movements/pigs/documents/new_owner_guide.pdf correct as at 4/2013 and www.defra.gov.uk/ahvla-en/disease-control/abp/food-feed-businesses/disposal-treat-use-milk-products/ correct as at 10/2013. The pig is capable of eating a wide range of feed ingredients. It is, however, important to provide a diet with the correct and optimum nutrient balance to ensure the animal can make the best use of its feed. Always take expert nutritional advice together with veterinary guidance, especially when producing diets for all ages of pig using by-products. These will mainly be liquid or semi liquid delivered in large tanker delivery quantities and requiring a liquid feeding system. This involves considerable investment and tends to be best suited to a medium- to large-scale pig production enterprise. These systems require very high levels of hygiene to achieve the best results, and this is easier to achieve with high throughputs of these nutrient-rich liquid diets.

ORGANIC PIGS

The fundamental principles of nutrition still apply to organic pig production. The UK organic pig producer must ensure that the animals only receive feeds that contain feed ingredients and additives as approved by the Soil Association. The Newcastle University Handbook on raw materials for organic pigs is also a useful reference; it is available from the BPA website in pdf format:
www.britishpigs.org.uk/Newcastle_handbook_of_raw_materials.pdf

Information on feed and nutrition in pig health:
www.thepigsite.com/pighealth/article/512/the-role-of-amino-acids and other feed components.

Further reading:
Kyriazakis & Whittemore *et al*, *Whittemore's Science and Practice of Pig Production* (third edition), Blackwell, 2006.
Close, W.H. and Cole, D.J.A., *Nutrition of Sows and Boars* (Nottingham University Press 2003, reprinted 2009).

4

The Pig and its Environment

The environment can be defined as everything that affects the pig's wellbeing and physical performance. It includes climatic, structural and social factors as well as nutrition, husbandry and health. Animal welfare must be paramount, but the process of converting feed into pig meat must also be as efficient as possible. Welfare and production efficiency can go hand in hand if the pig's climatic and housing environment is correct.

TEMPERATURE (THE THERMAL ENVIRONMENT)

Piglets emerge from the warmth of the sow's womb at a temperature of 39°C, and enter a world where temperatures may be in the teens or even less. Hopefully it will be around 21°C in a modern farrowing house or well bedded outdoor farrowing arc. If there are no heat lamps placed at the rear end of the sow indoors, a piglet's body temperature will fall by an average of 2°C within the first thirty minutes. If it survives, it may take up to ten days to return to normal in bad conditions. Such piglets are lethargic and fail to suckle, and/or they lie close to the sow and risk being crushed. The baby pig has a deep body temperature almost 1°C hotter than the sow, and it needs to keep this within a very narrow range.

In the first hours after birth, the baby pig requires air temperatures above 30°C. It will probably use food energy or body reserves to keep warm at temperatures below 32°C, but also it cannot cope with temperatures only a few degrees higher, when it will begin to use energy to keep cool. Piglets are very badly designed to cope with their thermal environment and radiant heat is very useful.

Once they begin to suckle and consume good quantities of food, their demand for warmth drops down gradually to around 24°C at three weeks of age. The actual upper and lower critical temperatures (UCT and LCT) are influenced by factors such as the amount of feed consumed, the size of the pig, group size (huddling), floor type, building structure, air speed and air temperature. A sharp rise in LCT and UCT coincides with the pigs being weaned; they usually stop taking in nutrients for a short time and then take several days or even weeks to get their feed levels back up again.

The sooner they begin to eat and grow, the sooner their LCT comes back down again. In a situation where the weaner accommodation temperature is controlled artificially, it is common practice to place four-week-old pigs in a lying area with an environment of around 26–28°C. This is then stepped down over three weeks to about 22 or 24°C.

Large pigs have lower LCTs than small pigs, and will lose less heat because of their relatively small surface area to body size. Groups of pigs huddling together will have less surface area to lose heat from and will have a lower LCT. Pigs kept above their UCT will attempt to wallow, will have reduced feed intake and growth rate, and may die if conditions are extreme. Air speed also influences the LCT and UCT. Although useful when it is very hot, rapid air movements resulting in draughts can add many degrees to the LCT. Radiant heat from either the sun or a heat lamp will allow pigs to be kept at a lower air temperature.

The Long-Term Effect of Cold on Weaner Pigs

Work at the Institute of Animal Physiology at Babraham, Cambridge produced some interesting results relating to the way temperature affects the growing pig. It was clear that the pigs kept at low temperatures were light for their age even when fed at a higher feed level, while the pigs kept at high temperatures were significantly heavier and converted their feed more efficiently. This was to be expected, but the most significant finding was the change in body composition. The animals in the cold had a rotund appearance with short limbs and tail, small ears, short snout and hairy skin. By contrast, those in the warm had an elongated appearance with a long tail, long ears and a long snout. The pigs had therefore adapted to their thermal environment, growing extra hair and developing a reduced surface area in the cold. There was even more hair on cold pigs fed a restricted diet.

It is also interesting to note that the actual body temperature of the pigs kept in the cold was lower than that of those kept in the warm. These findings underline the tremendous adaptability of the pig. Work done by Dr W. Close indicated that for every degree that

Example: Trobridge Monopitch Weaner Nursery Pen
Artificially controlled natural ventilation (ACNV) air flow

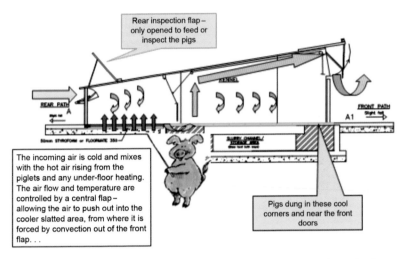

Rear inspection flap –
only opened to feed or
inspect the pigs

REAR PATH

TUNNEL

FRONT PATH

A1

50mm STYROFOAM or FLOORMATE 350

SLURRY CHANNEL / DUNGING AREA

The incoming air is cold and mixes with the hot air rising from the piglets and any under-floor heating. The air flow and temperature are controlled by a central flap – allowing the air to push out into the cooler slatted area, from where it is forced by convection out of the front flap. . .

Pigs dung in these cool corners and near the front doors

This monopitch roof example illustrates a very popular trend across Europe that maintains two temperature environments, for lying (26°C) and for exercise + dunging (>15°C). This makes efficient use of the piglets' own heat generation and is energy efficient.

Piglets indicating that the solid floored rear lying area is getting too warm. Some are using the semi-solid polymer slatted dunging area as a lying area. The internal manual flap requires adjustment using the fitted hand winch. The plastic strips can be easily removed in hot weather and for cleaning.

Principal ventilation systems in use in pitched-roof pig housing.

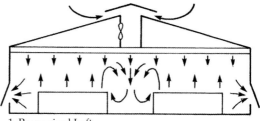

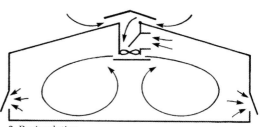

1. Pressurised Loft

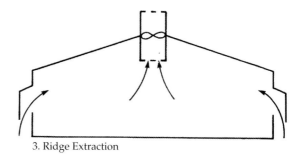

2. Recirculation

3. Ridge Extraction

a growing pig is below its LCT, it will both lose weight and require additional feed. These are known values, and we can calculate the cost of poor temperature control.

The pig can cope with relative humidity ranging from 60 to 90 per cent, so that is not normally a problem in practice; nor is lighting usually a problem in pigs, although there is evidence that pigs do well during summer lighting patterns. This is probably a good guide to controlling the timing of the daily lighting patterns. The optimum for breeding sows is considered to be sixteen hours of light at 200 lux. Suckling piglets may increase suckling when given fifteen to eighteen hours of light, and it may well be similar for finishing pigs. The code of recommendations for the Welfare of Pigs advises at least eight hours of daily supplementary lighting (40 lux) if natural light is not available.

Ventilation

The purpose of manipulating the ventilation rate is to control air temperature, relative humidity, air quality and air speed (draughts) at pig level. As pigs are so sensitive to temperature, it is usually used to determine ventilation rates. In mechanical or artificially controlled natural ventilation (ACNV) this ceases to be a satisfactory guide at very low temperatures when minimum ventilation is required. The problem with minimum ventilation is the risk of noxious gases building up; these include ammonia, carbon dioxide, hydrogen sulphide and carbon monoxide (if gas heaters are used or slurry levels are too high). Take expert advice if you suspect your minimum ventilation rates are too low. Maximum ventilation is more easily controlled.

Ventilation systems need to be designed well and checked regularly, so do take expert advice. They can be fully fan powered or fan assisted; pressurized (blowing in) or extraction; partial recirculation or completely natural. Every one of them must be installed, used, adjusted and maintained correctly. Controls may be completely manual, or may involve highly sophisticated computer systems. All mechanical systems must have a fail-safe device, including alarms, built in. Although ventilation is a complex science, most experts agree that inlet design and location is the most critical element, whilst the fan, where included, must ensure adequate air movement. As a guide, the air speed across a pig's back should not exceed 0.2m per second. Smoke devices can be used to estimate air speed and direction.

Dust is also a health hazard in pigs and humans. Try to avoid feeding dusty meal, and use industrial vacuum cleaners before every wet cleaning process.

THE STRUCTURAL ENVIRONMENT

The role of insulation in pig buildings is closely linked to the ventilation rate. There is no point investing in improved insulation if the ventilation system is not in order. 'U values' are quoted for insulating floors, walls and ceilings. The lower the 'U value' is, the better the insulation value. The 'U value' shows the heat flow through material, and different thicknesses of various materials will often produce the same factor. A good level of insulation will give a 'U value' of around 0.25, and compared to a 'U value' of 1.0 it will give between a 5 and 10°C temperature lift.

AREA REQUIREMENTS FOR PIGS

The current (EU Commission Report 2008) EU minimum required areas for pigs to rest and dung are listed below for weaner, grower and finishing pig housing, and include an estimate for the extra space required when pigs are kept to heavier weights compared to the weaner piglet:

Average weight	m^2	Extra space needed (%)
Up to 10kg	0.15	100
10–20kg	0.20	133
20–30kg	0.30	200
30–50kg	0.40	266
50–85kg	0.55	366
85–110kg	0.65	433
More than 110kg	1.0	666

See also www.gov.uk/pig-welfare-regulations

HOUSING SYSTEMS

Around 60 per cent of the UK breeding sows are kept indoors; the remaining 40 per cent are managed under outdoor systems. The outdoor system has maintained a higher share of the UK sow herd over the most recent decline in sow numbers, suggesting that there has been an economic advantage for this approach.

The sows are managed in groups during mating and pregnancy. Farrowing arrangements vary, but some of the smaller outdoor units run individual farrowing paddocks and huts. Larger herds can farrow sows in groups, but they each have a farrowing hut. The capital cost of setting up a breeding unit is lower outdoors and there have been financial advantages. The future challenge is to improve productivity at the same pace as the modern cost-effective indoor pig

Outdoor farrowing arc in winter, with piglet fender and door flap. This hut is insulated for winter warmth and summer cooling.

Outdoor farrowing paddocks in Oxfordshire.

unit can achieve. This productivity challenge, and the need to maintain a reduction in production costs, is central to the future success of outdoor pig production, just as it is for indoor housing systems.

The equipment required is based on two types of pig arc: one suitable for a single sow and litter, preferably with a fender designed to keep very young piglets in, and make it easy for escaped piglets to return; and the other a larger one suitable for mating, pregnant sows, gilts and boars. A number of manufacturers and designs are available based on corrugated/metal sheets and wooden construction. Tents are also used for sow accommodation.

Sows are kept in by electrified fences, and the field layout can be based on the paddock or radial system. The radial system allows sows, gilts and boars to be moved from one paddock to another in the central area. Feeding is carried out by driving around the outer perimeter and feeding large sow cobs or rolls. Good quality straw is essential in this system, especially in the farrowing arcs.

Piglets are treated in the same way as indoor piglets. Many of them come indoors at weaning, into housing similar to that used for indoor reared piglets. Stocking rates are around eight sows per acre (twenty per hectare), and ringing is often advised to avoid too much rooting in the soil. It is a system that requires hardy breeding animals, good, dry, free-draining soils, and excellent management. It fits well into an arable rotation.

Many outdoor pig farmers do not have a traditional tenancy, nor do they own the land, and they operate on a nomadic basis, moving on to fresh ground every one to two years. It is wise to avoid returning to the same field within eight years. Outdoor pig keeping has to be managed to the same high standards as indoor production, and sourcing top class advice and experience is essential.

Indoor pig housing had to change rapidly in the 1990s, from a situation where 60 per cent of the sows in the UK were kept in sow stalls or tethers, to a total ban by 1999. Group housing had to be introduced, and this system is now based on houses where computer-fed sows are recognized by electronic identification, with automatic floor feed dumping systems and sow-operated voluntary free access individual feeder and rest stalls. Where pigs are fed by computer, their identity and daily feed is monitored and programmed by the operator. Many sow yard systems also use individual feeders, in which sows can be fed once a day. Other systems include voluntary cubicles or stalls. The liquid feeding of sows in groups is also used effectively. (*See* Chapter 8).

In 2013 EU regulations stipulate an unobstructed floor space of at least 1.64m^2 for gilts, and 2.25m^2 for gestating sows. There are also specifications relating to group size, pen width/length, continuous solid flooring, and the proportion (15 per cent) that can be slatted for drainage. It is essential for all buildings to conform to these requirements, and expert advice is required to ensure that sows and gilts are kept legally. Many of the systems described in this book work best with a more generous allocation of space for sows and gilts than the prescribed minimum values.

Almost all indoor herds farrow in crates, although there has been a renewed effort internationally to develop effective 'freedom farrowing' alternatives that allow sows more opportunity to move about. The Midlands Pigs '360 Freedom Farrower' appears to be achieving good results in commercial environments. Nevertheless, the farrowing crate was instrumental in bringing the mortality rate of 25 per cent in the 1950s down to the 10 or 11 per cent more common in

Outdoor farrowing arc and newly born litter.

Outdoor weaner hut with deep litter (straw) and ad-lib feed hopper. These huts are moved and cleaned between batches; they are double-skinned, and have an insulation layer. Full width feed hoppers have proved to be one of the most efficient methods of feeding weaner pigs indoors and outdoors.

Outdoor weaner huts and runs in winter – water barrels are located outside in the deep-bedded dunging area on free-draining, sandy soil.

Tractor front-loader bucket filling a weaner hut feed hopper on an outdoor unit in winter.

Sow stall housing with automatic feeding in Belgium: it can only be used for the first twenty-eight days of gestation in some EU countries. It is banned in the UK.

the better indoor herds. There have been many innovations over the years, including the pronged crate and a hydraulic crate which restricts the sow when necessary but allows more freedom when she is lying down to suckle.

Piglets are usually catered for with a heat source, most commonly in the form of a heat lamp or dull-emitter bar heater. Electronic heat pads are available, and under-floor heating using hot water is common in Continental Europe. Heat lamps are excellent for keeping piglets warm, and because of the radiant effect, they warm up the body core well. They are essential during the piglets first few hours, regardless of any under-floor heating.

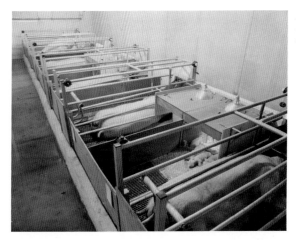

Farrowing house with covered side, forward creep and heat lamps.

Creep areas where the piglets can escape are now a standard fitting. There are forward creeps (most popular) and creeps at the side. Creeps can also have a lid covering the piglets. American scientists have suggested that a red light is best in the first twenty-four hours, after which a normal light attracts the piglets better. Carpet rests laid on the floor of the creep have also been recommended as they evidently produce a comfortable stimulation; also piglets will tend to return to carpeted creeps more readily and rapidly after birth, thus keeping them from harm's way. Side creeps are often preferred as piglets tend to use them sooner than forward creeps. All the time they are out of the creep they risk being chilled, or killed if the mother lies on them.

Midlands Pigs 360 Freedom Farrower can be used as a conventional farrowing crate or as a freedom version as shown above. It is a combination of straw and slats. This system was approved by the RSPCA Freedom Foods Scheme in 2013.
MIDLAND PIGS LTD

Midlands Pigs 360 Freedom Farrower – this illustrates how the sow can be confined like a standard farrowing crate for safe handling. The pen is modified easily within just a few seconds. FINRONE SYSTEMS LTD WWW.FINRONE SYSTEMS.COM

Inside an outdoor farrowing arc shortly after farrowing – note the excellent straw bedding. Good quality dry bedding is crucial to the success of outdoor farrowing.

Weaner pigs are housed in a wide variety of systems, sometimes depending on the age they are weaned. Kennels, verandas (pens enclosed with open-air dunging areas) or bungalows are used for pigs weaned up to five weeks of age, whilst totally environmentally controlled, heated flat decks have been used for the piglet weaned up to their third week. Two-climate weaner systems are becoming increasingly popular in Scandinavia and central Europe. A high proportion of these weaning houses also rely on supplementary heat for the weaned piglet. Straw-based weaner pools for older piglets are also effective, although the initial building costs can be rather high. Outdoor piglets are often weaned into straw-based outdoor huts and kennels, with a confined outside dunging area formed using hurdles around the run.

Typical 100-sow 5 week weaned unit farrowing at 7 day intervals

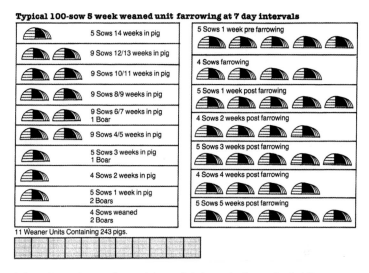

5 Sows 14 weeks in pig	5 Sows 1 week pre farrowing
9 Sows 12/13 weeks in pig	4 Sows farrowing
9 Sows 10/11 weeks in pig	5 Sows 1 week post farrowing
9 Sows 8/9 weeks in pig	4 Sows 2 weeks post farrowing
9 Sows 6/7 weeks in pig 1 Boar	5 Sows 3 weeks post farrowing
9 Sows 4/5 weeks in pig	4 Sows 4 weeks post farrowing
5 Sows 3 weeks in pig 1 Boar	5 Sows 5 weeks post farrowing
4 Sows 2 weeks in pig	
5 Sows 1 week in pig 2 Boars	
4 Sows weaned 2 Boars	

11 Weaner Units Containing 243 pigs.

Batch farrowing at three- to five-week intervals is increasingly popular, but there are implications for the number of dry sow, farrowing and weaner places. The larger batch size of sows and weaners increases the farrowing and weaner space required when batch farrowing every thirty-one days as compared to farrowing every week (seven days). As productivity increases, the number of weaners and weaner units will also increase, depending on how long the pigs are kept before being sold/transferred.

Typical 100-sow 5 week weaned unit farrowing at 31 day intervals

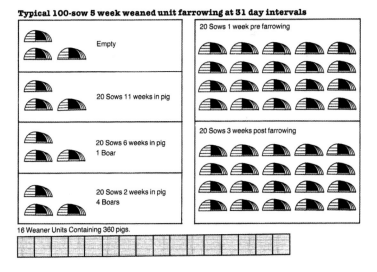

Empty	20 Sows 1 week pre farrowing
20 Sows 11 weeks in pig	
20 Sows 6 weeks in pig 1 Boar	20 Sows 3 weeks post farrowing
20 Sows 2 weeks in pig 4 Boars	

16 Weaner Units Containing 360 pigs.

Thirty-one-day interval. MASTERBREEDERS

Volume of Slurry Produced

Animal	Live weight (kg)	Litres/day	Litres/week
Weaner	15	1-plus	7–10
Grower	30	2	12–16
Finisher	70	4.5	30–40
Finisher	90	6	35–45
Dry Sow	125	4	25–35
Sow and litter	170	15	90–120
Boar	160	5	30–40

Finishing pig accommodation is also very varied, ranging from straw yards to slurry-based controlled-environment buildings. Monopitch 'Trobridge'-type houses are also very popular and can be straw or slurry based. Ventilation systems are best controlled by a climate computer, even if it is not fan ventilated and relies on 'controlled natural ventilation'. Finishing pigs outdoors may appear appealing, but there is usually a tremendous price to pay in increased feed costs, averaging around 30 per cent or more. It was estimated that only a small percentage (<3 per cent) of pigs were finished outdoors in 2012.

Dung and slurry disposal must be considered when planning a pig unit. The table [below] will be useful in estimating storage needs for liquid slurry. Solid farmyard manure (FYM) based on straw is more difficult to estimate.

The European Commission is due to complete a revision of the Integrated Pollution Prevention and Control (IPCC) publication – 'Best Available Techniques Reference Document v. 2' by 2014. The Environment Agency polices IPCC and currently (2013) all pig units with more than 2,000 pigs over 30kg, or 750 sows, are included in the scheme. In nitrate vulnerable zones (NVZ) locations where groundwater nitrates are high, there will be additional restriction based on slurry production. It is proposed (2013) for the legal requirement to store slurry to be at least five months and longer for some farms, for example NVZ location. There are also restrictions on when it can be spread. Liquid feed systems, and especially those based on milk by-products, can increase slurry production by 60 per cent or more.

Providing the pig with an adequate and cost-effective thermal environment is a challenge that can now be met in a number of ways.

Covered creep areas in the farrowing facility, two-zone thermal climate weaner accommodation, and energy-efficient and renewable technologies are examples that offer opportunities to improve the environment and production economics.

Straw-based systems clearly make up the highest proportion of the grower and finishing pig accommodation on UK farms. This is also true for weaner pigs, because the outdoor systems shown are almost certainly based on straw bedding. This is another unique feature of the UK pig industry compared to that in other EU countries. Good quality straw and its availability will remain a crucial aspect of maintaining this farm structure. It is also important for high welfare systems producing pigs under schemes such as Freedom Foods and Organic Production.

Outdoor breeding sows make up 40 per cent of the national herd and these also use straw bedding, along with many indoor-housed sows.

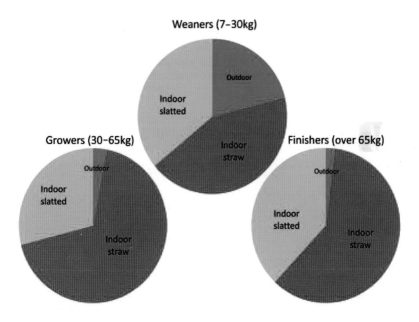

Types of housing found on UK pig units. BPEX 2013

View of a modern Trobridge monopitch weaner range incorporating solar panels and two grower/finisher rows. These have motor-driven ACNV flaps fitted front and rear, controlled by a Farmex control unit. The weaner pens (the row with the feed inspection flaps) have a two-thermal climate design and the grower/finisher ranges have a single ACNV air space under the monopitch roof. Energy (electricity) heating costs for these under-floor heated weaner units are regularly less than 40 per cent of those of a conventionally heated flat-deck weaner rearing unit. The units also comprise mainly recyclable materials.

These pigs are automatically fed dry feed stored in the silos. An above-ground slurry store is also located close to the service roadway along the base of the tree line on the far side. This allows for good 'bio-security' by avoiding the need for vehicle access for feed delivery and slurry disposal. A loading ramp for delivery and sale of pigs is also located on the roadside.

— 5 —

Reproduction

SOW PRODUCTIVITY

Sow output increased at a tremendous rate in the UK between 1970 and 2000. In 2013 many commercial herds across the world were already achieving production figures in excess of thirty pigs per sow per year. This has been achieved through advanced selective breeding, improved nutrition and sound management techniques.

However, the UK suffered a terrible setback in sow productivity and piglet survival rates during the early years of the twenty-first century. This coincided with the unilateral banning of sow stalls, swine fever and foot and mouth disease outbreaks, and severe financial difficulties through depressed pig prices and relatively cheap imports. This was then exacerbated by a porcine circovirus (PMWS and PCV2) infection that wiped out whole litters of pigs and also produced amongst others a 'wasting' disease in those that survived. However, control measures and improved management over a ten-year period have now led to the UK herd improving its output once again. In 1970 the average performance of recorded herds (MLC) was 15.5 piglets weaned per sow per year, in 1990 it was 21.5, and in 2010 similar recorded herds achieved twenty-three pigs indoors and twenty-one pigs reared in outdoor herds. This trend is continuing, but the UK faces a tough task to catch up with countries such as Denmark, where average production is already in the upper twenties for their indoor herds in 2013. The following graph illustrates this, using the key performance indicator (KPI) of pigs finished to slaughter per sow per year.

The initial surge in productivity between 1970 and 2000 resulted from a move to earlier weaning, coupled with the introduction of cross-breeding programmes, which exploit hybrid vigour (heterosis). Breeding from hybrid pigs began to develop and gather pace during the 1960s.

Modern domestic pigs breed all the year round with only some variation in fertility occurring during sudden hot spells, especially during the summer and autumn periods. The pig's reproductive cycle is regular, very reliable and easily manipulated by management. It makes good business sense to rear the maximum number of piglets per litter and to lose as few productive sow days as possible at any weaning age. Weaning piglets at four to five weeks of age is now the most financially viable approach. The optimum for most herds in 2013 would probably lie somewhere between twenty-eight and thirty-five days.

The UK herd is beginning to show an accelerated rate of improvement since 2010. It took ten years – between 1999 and 2009 – for the UK herd to recover to the same level of finished pigs sold per sow year. The graph clearly illustrates how far ahead the Danish herd has moved. The Danes had also already converted a high proportion of their breeding herds from stall housing to loose housing by January 2013. It remains to be seen how this change affects some of the other major pig-producing countries such as Germany and the Netherlands. It should also be noted that the UK has 40 per cent of the breeding herd outdoors, and this does create around a one finished pig per sow per annum handicap due to weaning fewer pigs per sow per year outdoors.

Although very early weaning was once heralded as the only way forwards, there is a biological limit. Also, there is considerable evidence that as lactation length is reduced (below twenty-eight days), the sow produces more litters per year, but produces fewer pigs

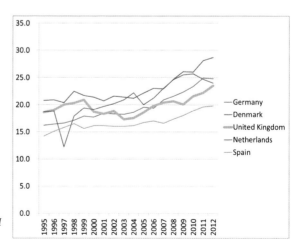

Pigs finished per sow per year in selected EU countries.

born alive per litter and conceives with greater difficulty, although in theory it requires less feed per piglet, per parity and per annum. Weaning sows at ten days or less after farrowing results in longer weaning to mating intervals, which can easily range from five to eighteen days or more within a single batch of sows.

It is currently an EU requirement that all piglets can only be weaned from twenty-eight days of age, unless there is an emergency, such as the sow being unable to feed them. It has been shown in very large-scale evaluated trials that weaning above thirty-five days neither benefits the sow nor the piglet, when compared to sows and piglets that suckle for twenty-eight to thirty-five days.

THE BOAR

Boars represent only about 5 per cent of the breeding herd in an indoor unit and up to 10 per cent of an outdoor unit, but they account for half of the genetic potential in the progeny. Therefore, they represent a significant investment each time a replacement is taken in (this is usually 50 per cent or more of the boars per annum). We have already discussed the importance of good, sound selection based on genetic and physical conformation – now we need to consider how to get the best from boars, or, in other words, manage them for maximum return on investment with minimum returns to service.

The average boar to sow ratio for indoor herds is around 1:20. If we accept a maximum farrowing index (litters per sow and gilt per year) of 2.5, then one boar will produce about one litter per week or fifty litters each year. If we accept 80 to 90 per cent farrowing to first service and perhaps 70 to 80 per cent for first returns, then one to two sows served per week would appear to be the normal average boar work-load. Mature boars can, and do, achieve heavier work-loads for short periods, but prolonged overwork, or indeed underworking with regular 'rest' intervals beyond two weeks, are to be avoided.

The Boar's Reproductive System

After puberty at six to nine months of age, the boar's ejaculate increases in both volume and sperm content until he is about eighteen months of age. The total ejaculate from a mature boar will typically contain between 20 and 80 billion sperms in 200 to 400 millilitres of semen fluids when given a four- to five-day rest between collections. A boar could keep this up for about five years, although it has been known for exceptional individuals to maintain this standard for eight to ten years. In commercial practice three to four years of age is rarely exceeded, since rapid generation turnover and genetic progress make it uneconomic to keep them any longer, regardless of semen performance.

A boar will produce 75 to 150 billion sperms per week, or up to a quarter of a million sperms per second, day and night. Each sperm takes thirty-five days to be made, and then needs a further ten days resting and maturing in the epididymis store before ejaculation. The sperms are produced in the seminiferous tubules, which make up a large proportion of each testicle. These tubules measure over 3km in a one-year-old boar, having grown from being just 29m at birth. There are probably a trillion sperms on the production line at any one time. Scientists have now produced evidence confirming the suggestion that the larger and more even the testicles are, the more fertile the boar is – a point well worth considering when selecting boars.

Heat Stress

The testicles are vulnerable to heat stress, and sperm production shuts down if the temperature of the testicle reaches 40.5°C (the normal body temperature is 38.5°C). There will be a time lag of fifteen days between the heat stress occurring and any apparent infertility. The thirty-four-day sperm production line and obligatory ten-day maturing of sperm before ejaculation, plus the fifteen days, suggests a sixty-day span before sperm production is back to normal again.

Other damage may also be caused which produces large numbers of abnormal sperms, and affects fertility. It is, therefore, very important to prevent heat stress caused by sudden increases in environmental temperature. A wallow works well for outdoor herds, or a water spray/shower indoors. Boars permanently in high temperature situations adapt by allowing the testicles to hang further away from the body, but a short term and sudden increase is too rapid for this adaption. However, even severe mange infection on the scrotum (the sack containing the testicles) could increase the temperature enough to cause infertility. A number of fever-causing diseases, such as swine erysipelas, will produce the same effect, so do not forget to vaccinate boars twice a year.

Even though a boar has this phenomenal potential for sperm production, overwork will speed up the production line and immature and deformed sperms will be the result. Damage could be severe, permanent and expensive. Continuous maintained overwork could well be the root cause of infertility in many boars.

A young boar keeps cool in very hot summer weather by wallowing in an outdoor paddock. In 2013 an ultra-modern JSR Pig AI Stud is reported to have installed air conditioning to maintain a constant 17°C environment.

Sows make efficient use of a muddy wallow and sun-screen netting to protect their skin against sunburn and also to reduce the effects of heat stress. This example is on free-draining soil and requires daily top-ups of water or a constant, cooling, fine low volume water sprayer (see below).

Low volume water spray.

A mature boar on a 1,700 sow breeding unit moves towards the farm manager and makes contact – an example and symptom of excellent animal-human interaction, despite this herd being virtually 100 per cent AI.

Puberty

As described, puberty in boars will typically occur at anything from five to nine months of age in the modern white pure-bred or hybrid. However, they should not be expected to make a regular contribution until they reach at least nine months of age. A boar's fertility level will usually improve quite quickly up to twelve months, and may continue on upwards towards two years of age. Generally we consider a boar to be at his peak at around eighteen months. It is now well proven, both scientifically and in practice, that a boar also increases his production of pheromones quite significantly during his first year of use, turning into a 'smelly old boar', producing large quantities of the all-important female-stimulating musk-like smell hormones in his salivary glands.

Training the Young Boar

Young boars are usually purchased from recognized breeders at around six or seven months of age (always check the age). You should always go for a boar that has been reared in a group, because it is well proven that boars reared in isolation from other pigs are less likely to work, and even when they do, they have reduced libido. Purchase a boar in plenty of time to allow for a period of isolation and acclimatization of a minimum of twenty-eight days (aim for forty days). This is designed to prevent him from bringing in any diseases or parasites, and to ensure he gets any vaccinations and other treatments due, prior to entry. If possible he should be given a disease challenge, by using pens formerly used by the herd's sows or fattening pigs, or by housing him for a few days close to, but never with, cull sows awaiting dispatch.

During this early period in the herd, time should be spent each day with the young boar in order to develop a bond that will help him settle in quickly and to form mutual confidence between him and the attendant. Once this period of isolation and acclimatization is over, he should be moved into a pen next to some young females – certainly not next to a mature boar! Allow him time to settle down, and keep up daily contact with him, especially as you lead up to his first service. Adopt a positive attitude, with the attendant playing the role of 'boss' animal, but with firmness and kindness. By this time he will be around nine months of age and ready for his first mating.

He may well work on his own, but if possible, arrange his pen so that he can see an older or more experienced boar working. This will arouse or certainly increase his interest, and reduce the chance of a failure on his first attempt. Choose his first partner carefully. There is no doubt that a first-litter, or a small second-litter sow is best, because she will be experienced but not too big. She should be brought into his pen, or, if available, a mating pen he is familiar with. Guide her to stand near the longest side, towards the wall, or pen division. Stay in the pen with him, but do give him room to go through the courtship ritual. Be ready to move the sow, using her tail if it is long enough, and make sure he can enter her vagina.

If he mounts in the middle or at the wrong end, don't panic. Wait a while and then gently shift him round if you can, but don't push him off unless the sow threatens to bite him. If so, gently lift over one front leg and let him slide off. If he mounts correctly, observe from a distance, and check that he is entering the vagina. Young boars can perform anal services, so check carefully. Once he enters and locks in the cervix, he will tend to stand on tiptoe, and as ejaculation commences, his anus will begin to pulsate, which indicates that he is pumping in the semen. At this stage, providing the sow and boar are standing well and performing normally, the attendant can stand clear.

Do not leave a young boar alone with the sow, because the sow could move into a difficult position and dislodge him. It is quite normal for some leakage of semen or clear fluid to occur. Also, quantities of a white gelatinous material which the boar uses to plug the cervix will be seen. Mating can take five or ten minutes, or longer, so be patient, and never push a boar of any age off before he is finished. He will often appear to withdraw and then lock in again with the characteristic tiptoe action. It is essential to ensure a non-slip floor; either deep litter or peat are ideal indoors. Avoid slippery concrete at all costs.

Natural service indoors – the boar mounts. Newsham breeding stock.

If a young boar fails to work, remain cool and try him with a different sow the next day, or as soon as possible. If this does not succeed, offer him a sow that has just been mated by another boar; it could do the trick.

Never put him in with a pen of gilts, as they can get very aggressive and could put him off for life. Try not to use young boars for heat detection, because they get frustrated. It is up to the attendant to detect when sows and gilts are on heat prior to offering them to young boars, in particular. Always check to see if he is lame, stiff or just generally unwell and do call the vet if in doubt. Once you have got him working, give him ten-day rests between his first three double services (mating on consecutive days).

Boar Work-Load

Once a young boar is working as described, do not exceed one double service per week (although some people triple serve

Three boars on an outdoor pig unit are giving their attentions to one sow showing the 'standing reflex'. One boar is mounting for mating whilst a second stimulates her with his nose. These boars were brought up together and work as a team. Never mix strange boars because they will fight, and this could cause serious injuries.
BOCM PAULS

successfully). Do not push it until he is thirteen to fourteen months old, when a rest interval of four (minimum) to fourteen days (maximum) should be aimed at. Experience shows that both conception rate and litter size drop if a boar is used constantly with less than four days' rest, and equally if under-used with rest intervals in excess of fourteen days. Do not forget, we are aiming for at least a two-year working life and 1,000 piglets from each boar – that is, 500 offspring per annum per boar. Outdoor herds operate boar teams of anything from two to six boars, but here the boar-to-sow ratio is lower at around 1:12, and so perhaps only 280 or so piglets per annum and 500 or so in his working lifetime are more realistic targets.

Always carry enough boars, use purchased semen, or carry out 'on-farm' artificial insemination to spread and maximize boar power. There is much evidence to support the notion that artificial insemination and natural matings mixed on the same sows increase conception rate and litter size. AI is sometimes practised for this reason on outdoor sows during and after very hot weather, or routinely during the summer months.

Keeping Records

It is essential to keep boar work-load records, and where possible, in both indoor and outdoor herds, a service register (paper or electronic) should be kept, noting all boars used on individual females. This can help avoid overwork and pin-point boars or boar teams outdoors that are performing below standard.

Safety

Boars can be dangerous and their tusks can cause severe cuts, even after the mildest of boars makes even so much as a slightly aggressive move. Take care, and use a pig board when necessary. Tusks can be removed, but this can cause libido problems for the boar, so you should take veterinary advice.

Feeding the Boar

Boars are often fed together with sows in groups, and it is important to ensure that they are fed correctly. It is very difficult to give exact figures for feeding boars, and they are tolerant of quite wide-ranging nutritional variations. However, there is evidence to suggest that inadequate feed in cold weather can lead to infertility. As a guide, 2.5 to 3kg of a sow's gestation diet (*see* Chapter 8) will be a normal level; increase the ration when they are working hard. Try and avoid them getting over-fat, because this will make them less eager to work and too heavy for many sows. This is almost impossible to achieve easily in outdoor herds because boars are in with sows during the period of high intake leading up to mating. Never use a boar immediately after feeding – it can kill him.

ARTIFICIAL INSEMINATION

Semen delivery service – or SDS – is the approach to pig artificial insemination now adopted by most farms in the UK. Pig artificial insemination centres no longer operate using an inseminator service, but specialists are available to advise on the correct techniques. Pig inseminations are carried out exclusively by farm staff, and are now the norm on most commercial pig breeding herds. Outdoor herds can also now use AI very successfully using various penning systems, often located under portable canopies/tents, to allow the good heat detection and insemination routines essential for its success.

Examples of two foam-tipped, and disposable and reusable 'Melrose' spiral-tipped catheters in common use. The type of catheter used is less important than a good technique and good timing of the AI.

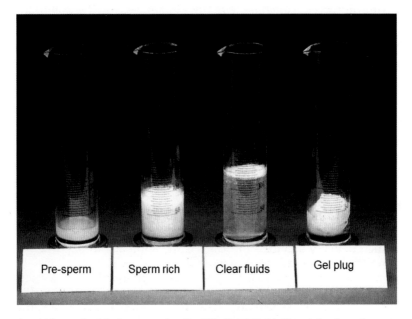

Pre-sperm | Sperm rich | Clear fluids | Gel plug

A typical example of the four semen fractions. The first 1–2ml is discarded and may be highly contaminated. The second 80–100ml is the sperm-rich fraction. The third 200–250ml is fluid from the accessory glands, which can make up part of the semen collected. The cylinder on the right contains the protein gel plug for the sow's cervix.

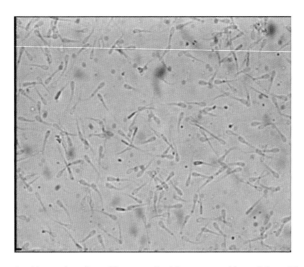

Boar semen should contain at least 60 per cent healthy sperms without defects. Most commercial AI centres set a 70 per cent target. Sperm motility (forward thrusting ability) is also assessed visually or electronically prior to clearing it for dilution into semen doses by adding it to the extender.

Semen is collected on farm after the boar has mounted a dummy sow. The semen is directed into a glass jar in an insulated flask via a sterile filter. The collector wears sterile, non-toxic disposable gloves for 'hand collection'. Good hygiene is essential, because contamination by bacteria and detritus will reduce semen viability and may result in the death of all of the sperm.

Semen Collection, Dilution and Storage

Artificial insemination stud boars are kept in locations well away from other pigs and in optimum environmental conditions. Rigorous health checks and quarantine periods are maintained. Although there are potential risks associated with disease transmission via artificial insemination, it is to be seen as a secure, high-health source of top quality liquid pig genetics. Unfortunately, boar semen does not freeze well. Individual boars can have their semen frozen, but often only about six effective doses can be taken from each collection (unlike the many hundreds possible from bulls). This makes freezing very expensive, and limits its uses to storing genetic material and to international transport and quarantine function.

Frozen pig AI litter sizes are also not commercially viable. It is a sad fact that many of the threatened rare breeds' semen does not freeze well, denying them this potentially excellent means of saving rare genes for the future.

Pooled or mixed semen has been used for commercial herds not involved in pedigree breeding. It was suggested that mixing the semen from two boars produces a boost in both conception rate and litter size. However, this is not considered to be a good practice because of the extra disease risk. Its efficacy was considered to be due to better sperm survival against the sow's immune system, which attacks foreign proteins such as boar sperm. About fifteen to thirty sows can be mated from one collection, and artificial insemination boars are used about three times per fourteen-day period, because this appears to produce the highest quality and quantity of sperm.

Boar semen is collected by holding the boar's penis in a rubber-gloved hand, although special artificial vaginas are also in use again in modern AI centres with exceptionally high standards of hygiene. The boar usually readily mounts a dummy sow, and semen collection can be learned quite quickly by both the boar and the semen collector. The semen is collected into a sterile glass container at 35°C, and is then inspected under a microscope to check how well the sperm move (motility). AI centres have long used semen density to estimate the sperm count per 1ml of collected semen ejaculate, based on sperm counts using microscopy. More advanced equipment and techniques have recently improved the accuracy of the sperm count used.

Most centres provide two doses of diluted semen to allow at least a double service for each sow. Two to three billion sperms are usually added to the diluent extender per dose. The semen is then stored at 'room temperature', 16–18°C. Semen is badly affected by slight increases in temperature above 19°C. The diluents render the sperm immobile so they conserve their energy until they are warmed up again during insemination. It may be a good idea to put a semen bottle or sachet in your pocket to warm it up and get the sperm moving again prior to insemination.

The diluted semen is delivered in insulated containers and should be stored in a purpose-built semen storage container set at a constant 17–18°C (min. 15°C – max. 19°C). Avoid temperature shocks at all times, and turn the semen gently daily to keep the settled sperm mixed. Store away from UV light (sunlight) as this will kill the sperm.

Timing the Insemination

Be sure to order semen in good time, and to combine this with good heat detection. The semen needs to be as fresh as possible. Use Monday's semen by Wednesday if possible, and Friday's by the following Monday morning. It should be inseminated at the optimum time. Semen extenders (usually based on EDTA) are good to keep semen viable for up to four days, and there are others available that claim to extend its life well beyond four days.

Heat detection for both natural and artificial insemination should be carried out twice a day. The number of days that a sow takes to come into oestrus after weaning can vary during the year, and is certainly quite variable between farms and in relation to the number of days the sow suckled. Always check sows for signs of them coming into oestrus from the day of weaning, especially if they suckled for thirty-five days or more. Sows that come into oestrus within four days of weaning will often have a longer heat (three days) as compared to sows that take six days or more (these often stand for less than two days). Some of the sows weaned on, for example, a Thursday will usually begin to exhibit a 'standing reflex' on the following Monday, and when they are well synchronized, all of them will have been inseminated by the following Thursday.

The first signs of the sow coming into oestrus are during what is known as her proestrus, which usually begins about a day before she will first 'stand' for the boar – however, it can last for one to three days. This means checking Wednesday/Thursday weaned sows on Saturday and Sunday, and recording their responses. If a sow did not stand in the morning but is standing in the afternoon, delay mating until the next morning, and AI again as late as possible on that same day. If a large batch of sows is being inseminated, it is worthwhile buying extra doses to cover some sows for a third time, or using a combination of a boar and artificial insemination.

The chart on page 113 indicates when peak fertility occurs in the sow. Sperm must spend about eight hours in the sow being 'capacitated' before they can effectively fertilize the eggs. Ovulation in the sow takes place about two-thirds of the way through the time she exhibits a standing heat in the boar's presence. This will be about thirty-six hours into oestrus in sows that have a standing reflex of two days, and closer to forty-eight hours in sows with an oestrus duration in excess of three days. In turn, the typical sixteen to thirty eggs released have a very short time period of a few hours when they can be fertilized successfully in both of the sow's oviducts (fallopian tubes). This makes precise timing difficult, and justifies why some sows need a third insemination if the initial two were considered too early. On larger units the PIGSIS system (PIG Simulation model for Insemination Strategies) can help pinpoint the best time to inseminate. It is worth considering mating gilts, returns to service and older sows three times (for example AM – PM – AM).

The boar is an essential part of the team in pig AI. The boar can be vasectomized for those situations where an accidental natural mating would prevent the sow from being mated with the boar or breed of boar required. Vasectomized boars can provide additional stimulation because they can actually mate with the sow or gilt. This should be part of his routine, to ensure that both he and a normal stock boar remain interested and maintain a good stimulating effect on the sows and gilts.

Weaned sows should have full boar contact for at least fifteen minutes a day for the first three days after weaning. Sows will respond better to a boar used to detect heat during the first twenty minutes or so after they are introduced to him. Once sows exhibit a standing reflex, remove them from contact with the boar and reintroduce them just before AI. Sows will sometimes respond better to the boar they have become familiar with, and the same applies to gilts. They can be frightened by a large aggressive boar, despite the fact that his pheromones are far more powerful than a young boar.

It has been proven that this boar stimulation actually increases the rate and intensity of uterine contractions in the sow. It is worth considering that the tiny spermatozoa have to travel the length of the 1.5m-long uterine horns, which is the equivalent of about 30 to 40 miles when scaled against a human, to reach the entrances to either of the two fallopian tubes (oviducts). They could not possibly swim there in time themselves, and are totally reliant on the semen flowing there aided by the sow's uterine contractions.

The sperm must rest at this entrance where they are capacitated for about six to eight hours and made ready to fertilize the eggs.

They then move on up to meet the ova (eggs) in the oviducts in each of the sow's two uterine horns, propelled by their tails and swimming against the tiny cilia conveying the ova towards them in the opposite direction. They remain viable for about twenty-four hours in the sow, whilst the eggs are no longer viable from about twelve hours or even earlier after ovulation.

Insemination should be carried out in the sow's normal surroundings, preferably with a boar in the next pen or in front of her, for example when in an AI service stall. The boar effect will only last for up to half an hour, and it is good practice to organize all inseminations during this time. On larger farms it is good practice to have a number of people carrying out the inseminations on groups of sows, as this avoids sows being inseminated once the boar effect wears off and ensures the inseminators maintain a high standard. In Belgium, sows on some farms have heavy sand-filled sacks placed on their backs during mating; if possible, sit on the sow whilst inseminating.

There are many different types of catheter in use, and virtually all are now disposable and very effective. Insert the catheter, taking care not to contaminate the tip (aids are available to ensure a hygienic insertion), having parted the lips of the vulva, and aim it towards the roof of the vagina in order to avoid entering the bladder and/or damaging the urethra. Make sure the vulva is clean, and avoid getting dirt on to the catheter.

The catheter should be lubricated with liquid paraffin or a product such as KY-Jelly, avoiding the hole at the end of the spiral or tip (most disposable catheters have no spiral). The traditional Melrose rubber spiral catheters are reusable, but you must make sure that they are completely dry inside as well as out before using again. Mixing water with the diluted sperm can kill it, so take care and always source expert advice.

Once inserted, turn the spiral catheter gently with the left-hand thread, which mimics the boar's penis, and push it in until it begins to lock in the cervix. It will then spring back in a clockwise direction. If you do not succeed at first, remove it and try again. During oestrus, the folds of the cervix become firm or turgid, enabling the boar's penis or any of the various catheter types to lock in. This helps prevent semen loss during both natural service and artificial insemination. Intra-uterine catheters are also available: these have a thin extension at the end, which passes through the cervix and deposits the semen dose directly into the uterus.

These intra-uterine catheters require more skill to use, and it takes longer to complete the insemination. A reduction in the number of sperm per dose to one billion or less has been attempted with these catheter designs. Expert instruction, advice and training are absolutely essential with this type of catheter.

Various devices are available to hold the semen container and catheter in place to allow the inseminator to AI a number of animals at the same time. These include a holder that clips or straps on to the sow's back and holds the semen container up to allow it to flow. The 'Automate' catheter has an integral semen sachet fitted around the shaft of the catheter, and this is inserted into the sow (*see* photograph). This catheter can be left in until all the semen has entered the uterus.

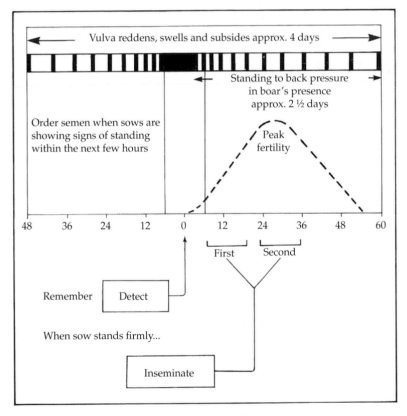

Order semen for animals likely to be standing in the next twenty-four hours

Detecting heat, ordering the semen and timing the insemination. PIG GENETICS

REPRODUCTION

The 'Automate' catheter being inserted into a sow in 'standing' oestrus. The blue part of the catheter is an integral sachet of semen which is released into the sow when a heat sensitive plug is released due to body heat. The catheter can be left in the sow until it falls out or is removed. The catheter is covered in a protective plastic covering that ensures it is clean when inserted through it. RATTLEROW FARMS LTD

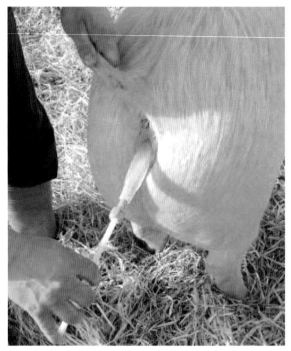

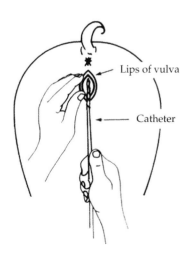

Lips of vulva

Catheter

Before insertion, the catheter must be lubricated.
PIG GENETICS

114

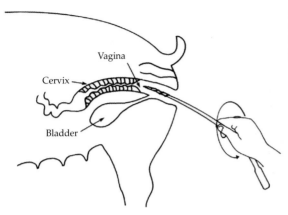

Once inserted, turn the catheter, gently mimicking the boar's penis. PIG GENETICS

Flatpack semen sachets are also available with non-toxic coloured dyes to ensure that the inseminator does not inseminate the wrong breed or hybrid boar semen.

Sexed semen is now a possibility and could become a commercially viable procedure when it is desired to have predominantly one sex in the resulting litters.

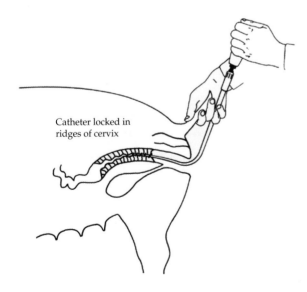

Bend the catheter shank up so that the bottle containing the semen is held higher than the vagina. PIG GENETICS

Turn the semen bottle or sachet several times, gently mixing the settled semen, and then cut the tip off the bottle prior to attaching it. Push this on to the end of the catheter. Bend the catheter shank up so that the semen container is held higher than the vagina, keeping the catheter locked into the cervix. Do not exert heavy pressure, but gently squeeze the container and help it to collapse as the semen is taken in. The insemination will normally take five to ten minutes, although it may take longer, especially with gilts. If semen leaks out, take out the catheter and relocate it in the cervix. Repeat the insemination sixteen to twenty-four hours later using a clean catheter.

If using a traditional rubber reusable catheter, flush it through and wash in clean water immediately after use. Never use any disinfectant or soap as this will kill the sperm. Sterilize in boiling water for at least ten minutes using the special trays designed for this purpose, or similar containers. As stated earlier, water kills sperm, so make sure that any excess water is shaken off. Flush through with distilled water and hang the catheter in a warm place to dry. Store in a clean polythene bag.

It is important to understand the AI process thoroughly, and to undertake training. Take plenty of advice and keep up to date. In 2013 BPEX had an excellent series of pdf leaflets available online,

A state-of-the-art AI semen collecting pen showing the artificial vagina (AV) and collecting flask. The cervix is mimicked and the AV has a gentle pneumatic pressure and cervix that can also be pulsed to mimic the sow's contractions. The person doing the collection stands in a pit and works at a comfortable level, ensuring safety and comfort for the boar and operator.
RATTLEROW FARMS

along with training videos to be viewed online and 'Pig Apps' on a smartphone or tablet. These are useful for both the new entrant and experienced practitioner alike. Access these at www.bpex.org.uk or practicalpig.bpex.org.uk. Pedigree pig breeders can obtain details of AI centres from www.britishpigs.org.uk/aisemen.htm. Commercial AI centres are operated by the breeding companies that supply breeding stock. Semen is delivered in flat packs via controlled temperature delivery services.

The BPEX AI Quality Standard was launched in September 2006. It is based on the evaluation of each step of the production processes for the collection and preparation of semen, and agreement on the 'best practice' standards. The five main British pig breeding companies (ACMC, Hermitage Seaborough, JSR Genetics, PIC and Rattlerow) were involved in its development: www.bpex.org.uk/downloads/300829/298983/KT%20Bulletin%208%20-%20AI%20Standard.pdf.

Artificial insemination is a bargain service where costs per sow service are similar to that of keeping an inferior farm boar. With good training and sound techniques, their reproductive performances will be at least equal. Do not miss the opportunity of attending training courses when they are offered.

DIY On-Farm Artificial Insemination

The procedure of collecting semen from boars, and inseminating sows on the same farm, is carried out on several farms in the UK. Farmers have their own small labs complete with microscope, and appropriate diluents (extenders) can be purchased for on-farm use. Many UK farms have applied this technique successfully, and it is an excellent approach on the larger pig farm, which can afford to buy a very expensive high-calibre animal.

It should be noted that it is illegal to sell or even give semen to another pig farm, nor is it possible for individual farmers to set up their own small artificial insemination service, because a Government Ministry licence is required.

THE FEMALE REPRODUCTIVE SYSTEM

The sow or gilt reproductive system is similar in outline to that found in all farm mammals. There are, however, a number of special features which the pig keeper needs to be aware of.

The Gilt and Puberty

The majority of UK pig breeds will reach puberty at around six months, unlike some of their Chinese cousins who can begin breeding as early as three months of age and when they weigh anything from 8kg to 40kg live weight. We can do a number of things to help get a batch of gilts on heat earlier, and together in a synchronized group. The two most effective methods are moving and/or mixing the group, and, perhaps more importantly, housing them next to a smelly old boar. Gilts will respond much more rapidly to a boar of

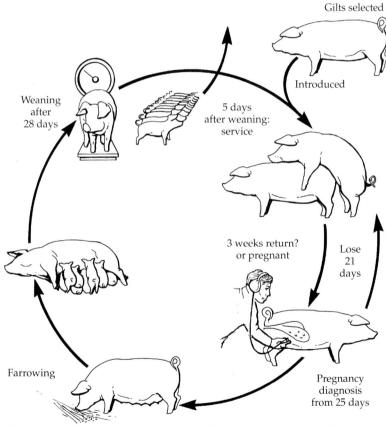

The sow cycle – 149 days: the maximum possible litters per sow per year = 2.45 when weaning at twenty-eight days and with less than 95 per cent farrowing rates.

sixteen to eighteen months of age and producing high concentrations of pheromones. Scientists have demonstrated that groups of gilts housed next to or exposed for short periods daily to an old boar will come into oestrus up to a month sooner than groups housed next to an immature breeding boar. The best type of contact is via vertical bars that allow touch as well as sight, sound and smell. The following responses to the boar's presence are for sows, but they also underline the importance of all of these stimulating experiences for gilts at puberty.

Percentage of Sows Known to be in Oestrus Standing to be Mounted

- In the presence of sows only: 59
- With boar sound, such as replaying a recorded boar voice: 71
- When boar odour was added: 81
- When sows could hear, smell and 'feel' the presence of a boar separated by a solid barrier: 90
- When the barrier was a barred gate allowing snout contact, that is sight, sound, smell and limited touch: 97
- When the sows were put into the same pen as the boar: 100

These figures demonstrate the difficulty of using commercial pheromone spray aerosols to replace a mature breeding boar. When detecting oestrus in gilts, it is very important to allow sufficient time to complete the task effectively. The following are typical times required to detect heat in gilts.

Standing to back pressure within sight, smell and sound of a boar. PIG GENETICS

119

Outdoor sows and boar with direct contact in a tent-roofed outdoor AI mating area. This allows good use of the boar's smell hormones – pheromones – and shows one pen on each side of the boar pen with two to three sows only per inseminator. Note the sow in the far pen is allowing the person doing the insemination to sit on her back – this is the 'standing' reflex. The 'Automate' catheter is also being prepared. RATTLEROW FARMS

Time Taken for a Mature Boar to Detect Gilts in Oestrus

Minutes	<5	5–10	11–15	16–20	21–30	>30
Percentage of gilts detected	53	15	7	8	4	13
Cumulative percentage	53	68	75	83	87	100

These figures suggest that we should allow up to thirty minutes in checking a group of gilts. In the case of individual animals, we should certainly allow twenty minutes to achieve high detection rates. A gilt not inseminated as planned will cost as much as a missed sow if fitted into a herd replacement programme. Gilts should be gradually introduced to mature boars prior to their first mating, as this will reduce the response times considerably.

Fixed-Time AI

Hormones can be used to 'fix' the timing of ovulation and therewith the possible use of 'fixed-time AI' in batches of sows and gilts. This is particularly useful in larger herds practising batch farrowing. However, these hormones should only be considered for application

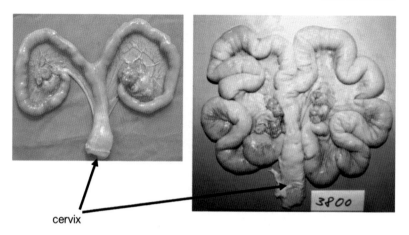

cervix

The left-hand picture shows the uterine horns of the gilt at puberty compared with the larger sow uterus. (The grape-like right and left ovaries are clearly seen.) Special gilt catheters are available for both standard and deep insemination – the gilt has a smaller and shorter cervix than the sow. J. KAUFFOLD, UNIVERSITY OF LEIPZIG

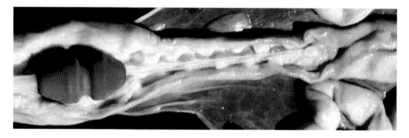

This catheter is an example of an intra-uterine version with a foam tip. It clearly shows the folds of the cervix, which the boar and the various catheter tips 'lock' into during the insemination process.

in herds with a high standard of management, and they must produce a good return on the initial outlay to justify their use.

Gilts need to have their oestrous cycle synchronized to fit into a batch farrowing system, and this can be achieved using a product such as 'Regumate' (altrenogest, a synthetic progestagen), which is administered as a palatable foam spray on the individual feed of each gilt in the group for eighteen days. When stopped on day eighteen, the gilts will be at the same point in their oestrous cycle and can then be allowed to come into oestrus just like a group of weaned sows. Alternatively they can have their oestrus and ovulation synchronized for the same day using either a treatment based on FSH (follicle stimulating hormone) and LH (luteinizing hormone), or more recently using Maprelin, which is a synthetic GnRH (gonadotropin releasing hormone) to replace the FSH. Insemination of both sows and gilts can then be planned at a fixed time. Farrowing will also occur within a defined time frame for each batch, and this can also be induced to synchronize births for a time and date that ensures maximum supervision and care for the sows and piglets. This approach must be carried out under expert veterinary prescription, supervision and closely monitored working practices.

Pregnancy Diagnosis

Ultrasonic devices are now undoubtedly the most popular method of pregnancy diagnosis in the pig. There are various types of ultrasound in use, and these include the ultrasonic scanner and the 'doppler'. The simplest ultrasonic scanner technique measures the echo returned from high-frequency (ultrasound) waves. A pregnant womb is full of fluids from about day twenty-eight and up to around sixty days post mating, and these produce an echo which indicates pregnancy. These machines are usually completely hand-held and have a probe which is lubricated with a sonic coupling gel or liquid and placed on the flank of the sow or gilt to be tested. If pregnant, there will be a tone and/or a light will glow. Scanners produce a cross-section screen picture (*see* photograph) and are an increasingly popular PD device. These can also provide 'real time' moving images, but this is not a requirement to simply confirm a PD+ result.

The well proven Doppler units come with headsets, and an ultrasound probe is placed in a similar position as the other methods on the flank and pointed at the womb. This time, the ultrasound waves are designed to bounce back from moving objects such as blood cells in the uterine artery. In the pregnant animal the uterine (womb) artery swells up rather like a balloon, and each time there is a pulse, it expands along its wall rather like a wave. This wave-like motion of the blood is called fremitus and indicates pregnancy. The Doppler headset presents the user with the characteristic 'whooshing' sound produced by fremitus. These methods will usually work well outside the body from day twenty-five up until farrowing, picking up the very rapid heartbeats of piglets from around day forty through to farrowing.

Both the simple pulse-echo and the Doppler are reasonably accurate, although the Doppler is probably favoured because it rarely gives false positives and works even during farrowing, where it is

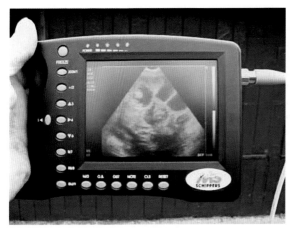

Schippers Scanner ultrasound pregnancy machine showing attached embryos in the dark uterus cross-sections at twenty-eight to thirty days after insemination. A positive pregnancy diagnosis (PD+).

useful to check if any more pigs are on the way. A Doppler rectal probe can be used to test for pregnancy as early as eighteen days, although this is of academic interest in most instances. The work done by scanners is referred to as 'sonography', and the more advanced machines can be used to check for disorders such as metritis in the uterus, and can even monitor ovulation. They can also be used to check the boar's testicles. These applications are currently used by specialist veterinary scientists and require skilled interpretation (*see* Kauffold, Wehrend and Beynon, *Pig International* 09/2010).

For early pregnancy diagnosis it is possible to take a tiny drop of blood and analyse the progesterone hormone level between day seventeen and day twenty-four post mating. Time and practicality are limiting factors, and these tests have not found favour on commercial farms, even though they have been potentially available for nearly thirty years.

It is important to consider that, although we can detect a PD+ after about twenty-one days, the sow can totally 'reabsorb' a litter up to thirty-five days of gestation. Death of the foetuses after this stage usually results in abortion or, more commonly, 'mummified foetuses'. The stage they died at can be estimated by measuring their length from the crown of the head to the rump, compared to an age scale.

Always re-check PD+ sows and gilts after thirty-five days to confirm pregnancy.

Farrowing

We now believe what the midwives of old always knew: the baby will arrive when it is good and ready. Scientists now tell us that the trigger that sets off the birth process is controlled by the foetus(es). Pregnancy (gestation) in the pig lasts for an average of 115 days, and in many trials there were few which exceeded 120 days or fell below 112 days. This is fortunate, because we can make then sure that our sow or gilt is already in the farrowing area when the signal for farrowing commences.

Hormones are released from the glands at the base of the piglets' brain, and these, in turn, eventually stimulate the placenta to send out a signal hormone called prostaglandin, which travels across to the mother's bloodstream, switching off the progesterone-making yellow bodies on her ovaries. These have been pumping out the hormone that maintains pregnancy for 110 to 115 days. The action of prostaglandin is unseen, but nonetheless quite spectacular. In minutes it has travelled to the ovaries and switched off these progesterone factories. Prostaglandin is equally quickly destroyed by the sow's body, and in minutes all traces of it are gone.

The short lifespan and speedy action of this hormone will trigger the birth process, or abortion if given artificially too early. In fact we now have a number of commercially available prostaglandins, along with gonadotropin-releasing hormones (GnRH), which can be administered by injection to induce birth if so desired under veterinary supervision. Birth usually takes place twenty-six to thirty-two hours later in the majority of treated animals, allowing attendants to be on hand and to save more piglets. Never inject a sow or gilt before day 114 of pregnancy because the piglets grow rapidly during the last days of pregnancy and could be born too early and too small to thrive.

Signs of Farrowing

It is important for the livestock attendant to be able to predict the onset of the second stage of farrowing, because it is then that assistance can prove useful. The possible indictors are:

Abdominal contractions: These will appear one to three hours before birth, although they can occur just fifteen minutes or up to ten hours before birth – as such this is not terribly helpful.

Bed or nest making: The pig is an intelligent and adaptable animal and it will generally only make a nest when it needs to. This takes place up to twenty-four hours before the first piglet arrives, so it is not a useful guide as to when birth will commence.

Increased restlessness: This is related to bed making or generally moving around, and is difficult to observe.

Expulsion of blood-stained fluids: Only about 40 per cent of sows actually discharge any fluids prior to the birth of the first pig. Of those that do, about 60 per cent will farrow within 100 minutes and about 90 per cent within two hours. This is a useful sign. Once seen, note the time and expect pigs within an hour or so.

Discharge of meconium (small greenish pellets expelled in the fluids before the birth of the first pig): Expect to see a pig within the hour. Twitching of the tail is another sign and usually begins a maximum of two hours before the first pig is born. During farrowing it often precedes the birth of a piglet by a few minutes or even just seconds.

Change in the rectal temperature: The sow's body temperature tends to rise by about 0.5°C just before farrowing. However, this is not a good indicator of the beginning of farrowing.

Making an udder and the presence of milk: There is often sufficient milk in an expectant sow's udder to squeeze out a jet up to twenty-four hours before birth. Milk is usually present within eight hours of birth. Gently rubbing the udder is a useful exercise just before farrowing, as the normal sow will respond by lying on her side and presenting her udder. If the sow is upset, then adrenalin is released and milk let-down by the hormone oxytocin is blocked – so be calm and help the sow relax. The presence of milk is not a good indicator of immediate farrowing as it can sometimes be seen several days before the event.

Other factors to consider when assessing the time of birth are the vulva swelling, relaxation of the pelvic ligaments and dropping of the

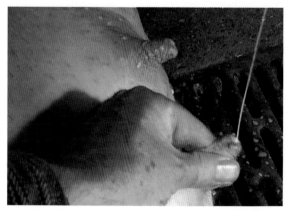

Checking for milk just before farrowing. Note that there are usually two orifices and sometimes three – though only one can be seen operating here.

125

REPRODUCTION

The first piglet captured using a high speed camera – they are often expelled very quickly.

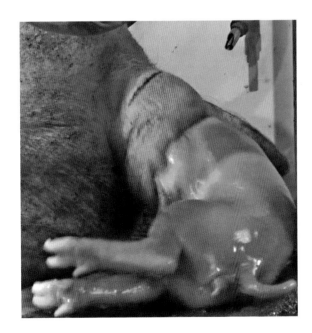

Backwards goes just as well.

udder. If it were practicable to measure them, the pulse and respiration rates will also increase. The farrowing attendant must learn to put some or all of these signs of farrowing together and to make a prediction. At the end of the preparatory stage, the cervix will have expanded and the pelvic girdle relaxed under the action of the hormones oxytocin and relaxin. This turns the uterus and vagina into one continuous tract, allowing the piglets to pass out during the birth process.

The second stage of labour is initiated by the first piglet pressing against the pelvic inlet (the passage through the pelvis). This starts up the voluntary contractions of the sow's diaphragm and abdominal muscles, and the piglet is usually expelled quite quickly. Contractions in the sow and gilt are limited to the area from the cervix out towards the vagina. It is important for the piglets to be expelled quickly once the water bags burst as they pass through the pelvic girdle; many piglets may die at this stage, from suffocation.

Manual assistance is needed less frequently with pigs than with other farm animals, but it is very important to know both when and how to assist sows and gilts during birth. The normal time taken for this second stage of labour is one to four hours. It is complete when all the piglets (alive and dead) are expelled and the afterbirth begins to appear. It is important to note that, on occasion, the afterbirth does come away in pieces between the birth of piglets.

Piglets are frequently born hind legs first, and these appear to be as viable as those born head first. In numerous student observation studies around 60 per cent were born head first and the remainder feet first. The average time between piglets was fifteen minutes, but the range was quite tremendous – it is not unusual in practice for four piglets to be born within seconds of each other.

As a general rule you should become concerned if a period of forty-five minutes has elapsed following the birth of the first piglet

Two born together –
one with the umbilical
cord still attached.

The urge to get to the udder is often immediate – the piglet in front still has its cord attached and it is almost on the udder.

The piglet is clearing its airways, as indicated by the mucous bubbles on its mouth and evidence of meconium (faecal dung) on its face and shoulder. Meconium indicates that it or another piglet has suffered partial suffocation (anoxia) during birth.

and there is no sign of the next piglet, or at any point beyond this in the birth order. On average, most farrowings are complete within two to three hours, but normal birth can last up to eight hours. The longer it takes and the older the sow, the greater the risk of piglets being born dead. There is a tendency for the gestation period to be up to a couple of days shorter with very large litters, and longer with very small litters.

Assistance During the Birth Process

If there is a delay of more than thirty to forty-five minutes after the first piglet, then you should investigate. First, check the sow or gilt and stroke the udder. If it is hard and the animal is feverish, then take its temperature: it should read around 38 to 39°C. If it rises above 39.5°C, then action will be necessary because you could be

Reaching the udder quickly to find a teat and take in colostrum.

dealing with the early stages of a disease and management syndrome known as MMA (metritis mastitis agalactia), where temperatures can reach 42°C. This is a complex infection of the womb and udder which can lead to lack of milk and the loss of all piglets.

If it is prescribed and available, inject oxytocin to release the pressure on the udder and help contract the womb and expel the piglets. On many occasions this also brings down the temperature and avoids the need for antibiotic treatment of MMA. Always carry out these procedures in consultation with your veterinary surgeon, and use the correct dose rates and injection sites. Oxytocin should be used with care and under strict veterinary supervision – it is now also available in a long-acting form. Constipation may be aggravating the problem, and feeding bran or a laxative diet for a few days before farrowing may help reduce the risk of future problems. Exercise is also very beneficial.

If the animal continues to have difficulties, then manual assistance may be necessary. The diagram on page 130 illustrates possible

Assisting the birth. PIG
INTERNATIONAL

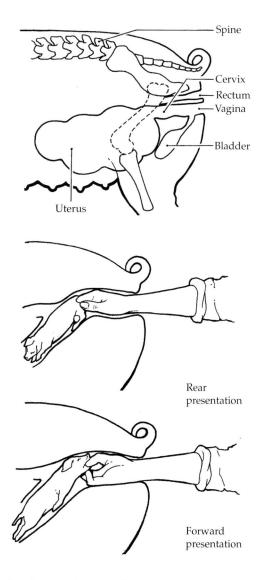

Spine

Cervix

Rectum

Vagina

Bladder

Uterus

Rear
presentation

Forward
presentation

presentations and methods of extracting a piglet. Always wear a disposable plastic full-length glove, and be prepared to use your arm beyond the elbow. Be sure to use a suitable antiseptic barrier cream, which will also lubricate the vagina especially if not using a disposable glove. Clean mains water also makes a good lubricant for

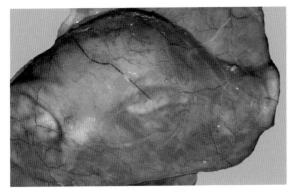

This piglet was born completely covered by the foetal membranes. Immediate removal by the farrowing supervisor got the piglet breathing and it was suckling the sow's udder within minutes.

disposable plastic gloves. Good hygiene is essential. Your veterinary surgeon will advise you, and in most instances will recommend routine antibiotic treatment following manual assistance.

In a good fertile herd an average of 4 to 6 per cent of the total piglets born will be dead at birth. In other herds this figure may be as high as 10 or 12 per cent. These stillbirths fall into two broad categories: the first group consists of those piglets that have been dead for some time prior to farrowing. These are more common in older sows, larger litters, or in premature births and in the presence of certain diseases. They can normally account for anything from 5 to 20 per cent of the total number stillborn.

The second group, which usually accounts for at least four out of five piglets born dead, is made up of those that die during farrowing.

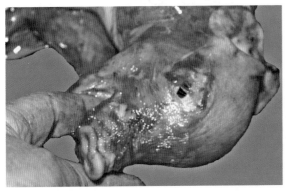

A finger is used to gently help the same piglet clear its airways of mucus and to start breathing on its own.

131

A piglet exhibiting typical signs of anoxia – gasping for breath. It recovered quickly and moved towards the udder to suckle. The front feet of this piglet also illustrate the soft 'slippers' on the clays designed to protect the uterus and birth canal from puncture by the sharp feet. Piglets dead at birth will usually still have these 'slippers' attached.

These piglets have probably suffocated, and will frequently show small green or brown dung pellets on their skin or in their ears. This is known as meconium or 'first dung', and it is believed that piglets pass these when they undergo trauma during suffocation after their umbilical cords break prematurely during birth. Some of these piglets survive at first, but die later due to brain and other organ damage caused by oxygen starvation (anoxia). Once again, this problem is greater in older sows and very large litters.

There is probably another category of stillborn piglets, which may account for as many as 50 per cent of those recorded dead at

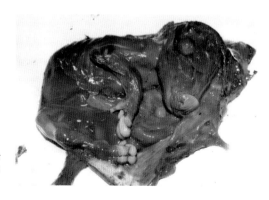

Close-up of a mummified foetus that died in the later stages of pregnancy.

The afterbirth is usually expelled quite quickly after the birth of the last piglet, but it is sometimes expelled in sections between piglets or groups of piglet. The act of suckling and the natural release of oxytocin by the sow is believed to assist in its expulsion. Always check that the sow has expelled the afterbirth (cleansed).

birth: these are those piglets often found dead entangled in the foetal membranes or even parts of the afterbirth, or chilled by cold wet fluids in an unheated maternity area, or in the absence of warm dry bedding. Using surgical gloves and a scalpel, remove the lungs from suspect piglets. If the lungs sink in a bucket of water, the piglet failed to breathe, but if they float, it most certainly took at least one breath.

It must be said that sows farrowing outdoors in arcs or in a less restricted farrowing pen tend to have fewer farrowing difficulties compared to those housed in farrowing crates. In general, it can be stated that the sow is much less troublesome during the birth process than other farm animals, but supervision of farrowing and assistance for individual piglets will always pay dividends. The piglet demands top-class management and care if it is to enter the world in a viable state to both survive and thrive up to weaning and beyond.

— 6 —

Piglets – Survival, Growth and Development

The survival chances of piglets are often fixed before they are born. Their birthweight has a dramatic influence, and piglets weighing less than 0.8kg have less than a 50 per cent chance of surviving through the first forty-eight hours unless intensive care is provided.

Heat lamps are an essential item when farrowing indoors, and it is well worthwhile having up to three available – one immediately behind the sow and one on each side of the farrowing crate. The smaller the piglet is, the nearer to its body temperature (38°C) it needs to be kept. As a guide, most new-born pigs kept in still air need an air temperature of around 29°C; this can be reduced to 22°C or so at weaning. Canadian research work has demonstrated that not only do piglets die more rapidly if cold, but of those that survive, growth rates are affected. Pigs kept in a farrowing room at a chilly 13.5°C gained 135g per day compared with 170g per day in those kept at 20.5°C during the first week of life. This could make all the difference between the development of a strong weaner and an inefficient nutritional runt. You should aim to produce piglets weighing at least 1.3kg at birth, a factor we can influence through good sow feeding and nutrition.

Outdoor-born piglets can be lost to predators as they are born in the farrowing arc (foxes are certainly involved – less likely badgers and dogs). Electric multi-strand 'Fox fencing' has been used successfully on many farms to reduce losses that were found to be between 2 and 10 per cent of piglets born.

PROBLEMS AT BIRTH

If the sow has had a long and difficult farrowing, the piglets may have suffered from partial suffocation if the umbilical cord broke several minutes before the piglet was expelled and could breathe in oxygen. Oxygen starvation may cause brain damage, or certainly a reduction in the piglet's energy reserve. About one in five of pigs born have the cord broken when they are expelled, and in general, these appear more exhausted and take longer to suckle than those born with the cord still attached. In the remainder, it takes about three or four minutes for the cord to break after birth; it will do so of its own accord, so unless the piglet is in danger, never break the cord. Some piglets may even get round to the udder with the cord still attached. There are more piglets born with broken cords amongst the later piglets born. It is interesting to note that these later born piglets run a greater risk of being stillborn.

Navel bleeding may be a problem in some herds, so do keep an eye on this. If it does occur, then tie off or clamp the cord, using sterile twine or clamps, and dip it into iodine solution, or spray with an antiseptic, especially if the herd has a persistent joint ill/navel ill problem. Prostaglandin induction will help up to 70 per cent of farrowings to take place during the working day. Use this to allow supervision and to treat navel bleeding until a cure is found, if it is not standard procedure. Wood shavings used as bedding in farrowing houses have also been implicated. If this is the case, then try using clean chopped straw. If the navel bleeding problem persists it may be cured by feeding the sow a teaspoonful of vitamin C (ascorbic acid) for the last four or five days before farrowing. (Riboflavin deficiency has also been recorded in navel bleeding episodes.)

If a piglet fails to breathe, check for a heartbeat by placing a finger gently on to the ribcage. Piglets have a very rapid heartbeat (200-plus beats per minute as compared to the sow's seventy to eighty per minute). If the heart is beating, try to get the piglet to breathe by clearing the nose and mouth of all mucus. Swing the piglet gently, holding on to the shoulder to help clear any lodged mucus. It will usually respond, but 'coughing' air gently on to the back of the throat through a tube may help. Do not blow too hard as this could damage its delicate lungs. It will not work every time, but many piglets can be saved in this way. Dry the piglet off quickly and place it under or on a heat source, especially if it is weak, in order to conserve its energy. If in a farrowing nest or an outdoor arc, place it amongst the other piglets to keep up its body temperature.

Sometimes a gilt or, less commonly, a sow may savage its own piglets, and this is a problem demanding prompt action. The pain a gilt probably undergoes at farrowing may make it aggressive. Keep piglets away from the mother's head, and do not leave them on the sow unless you are present. Keep them in a crèche until she calms

Layout of creep heating trials at Aberdeen University

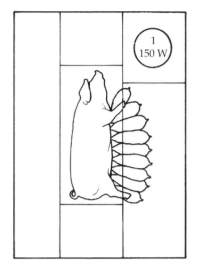

Basic

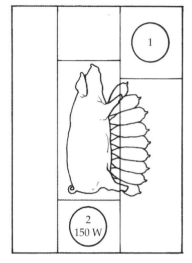

Intermediate

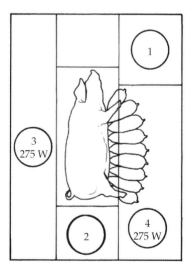

Luxury

Lamp 1 on continuously in all three cases. Lamp 2 on for 24 hours from farrowing. Lamps 3 and 4 on for 48 hours from start of farrowing.

down. Injections of a tranquilliser drug (Stresnil) combined with oxytocin may help. There is evidence that oxytocin helps encourage mothering instincts and milk let-down, and strengthens contractions. Do watch out for savaging, as it can be a costly problem.

SUCKLING

Piglets have a very strong instinct to reach the udder, and on average, they will have suckled within forty-five minutes of birth, although first-born piglets often take longer than those born later. They will probably have blurred vision at birth and find their way by touch, following the natural flow of hair which directs them to the udder. It is essential for them to receive colostrum containing antibodies from their mother's immune system, which may have been primed by vaccinating the sow against specific disease-causing organisms such as *E. coli*.

The sow milks almost constantly upon demand under the influence of oxytocin during farrowing and for the first few hours. Canadian research workers have found that piglets consume, on average, 100ml of colostrum within the first hour of life – in one instance an individual piglet consumed 90ml within ten minutes of birth. Unfortunately, many piglets do not suckle soon enough, and by the time they do, they do not get sufficient immunity. The milk changes its constituents very quickly during the first twelve to twenty-four hours: the level of protein containing the colostrum antibodies drops, and the piglet's ability to absorb them is lost quite rapidly, so it is important to get them to drink soon after birth. It is a good idea to collect colostrum from farrowing sows for freezing in small quantities; this can then be defrosted and warmed up to blood temperature for feeding to weak piglets via a 20ml syringe put into the mouth, or a stomach tube. It is important to be taught how to use a stomach tube, which is best lubricated with corn oil prior to insertion.

The importance of good teats has already been emphasized: a long teat well exposed and easy to hang on to is what every piglet searches for. More piglets will suckle front teats than rear teats. During behavioural studies of litters carried out by college students, it was found that there was an 80 per cent chance of one of the three or four teat pairs in front of the navel being suckled, compared to between a 20 and 40 per cent chance of the rear seventh or eighth teat pairs. On average, the piglets on front teats grew more rapidly than those on rear teats. Front teats are longer and more easily located on the bottom row, especially in older sows with a well stretched udder.

It was also noted that each piglet chose and kept to its own teat within the first days from birth. Researchers believe that once chosen, they find their teat chiefly by smell and touch. Using experimental rubber udders the piglets found their own teat even if it were moved to an alternative position. They will defend the teat quite fiercely, and if they are not tooth-clipped at birth they can inflict considerable damage to each other and possibly their mother's udder, leading to infection of their head, jaw and mouth, and possibly to mastitis in the sow.

Within a few hours of birth, the sow will normally begin to settle into a routine, suckling about once every forty-five minutes, gradually extending this to about once every hour after a few weeks. Energy reserves in a weak piglet are very low and, unlike many other mammals, the piglet will not last twenty-four hours without nutrient intake; thus every feed missed is a severe blow to a small and/or weak piglet. To add to its difficulties, the period of milk flow or let-down lasts only about 15sec, which means that it has no more than a few minutes to drink 4 to 5 per cent of its daily intake.

Piglets will drink twenty-four to thirty times per day, and during the first week a sow will usually produce about 5ltr of milk a day.

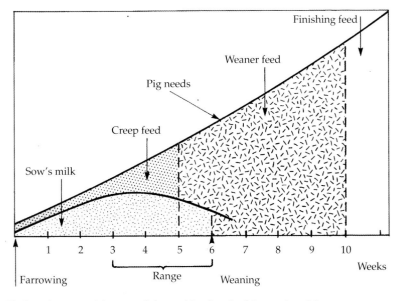

The lactation curve of the sow and the nutritional needs of the growing piglet. GERMAN AGRICULTURAL SOCIETY

Assuming that ten piglets are suckling, we would expect the average piglet to drink about 500ml per day in the first week. If it drinks this in twenty-five separate feeds, it must drink at least 20ml per feed. By the third week, the sow's daily milk yield will be 10 to 15ltr per day, and each piglet will consume about 1ltr or more per day. It takes at least 4ltr of milk to produce 1kg of piglet growth. If piglets are kept on the sow beyond the third week, then supplementary feed is necessary as the piglets' needs grow and the milk yield of the sow begins to fall.

Suckling and its Effects on the Mammary Gland

If a teat is not sucked sufficiently during the first twelve to fourteen hours post farrowing, then what is known as 'involution' occurs and the gland will have a severely reduced milk yield or may 'dry up' completely. Some recovery will occur if the teat is suckled within a day of farrowing, but this will be irreversible if it is not sucked during the first three days. This also appears to reduce that teat's output potential in the next lactation, though it is not known whether this affects the teat and gland in later lactations. We also do not know how long a teat needs to be sucked to maintain full output in the next lactation, for example should a piglet die.

Fostering

Fostering piglets is carried out in a variety of forms, of which about nine are known to the author, although there are at least twenty named fostering techniques. Fostering should be carried out as soon after birth as circumstances allow. Both sow and piglets learn to recognize each other, probably by smell, very soon after birth. Straight fostering, or evening up the numbers suckled between sows immediately after birth, is probably the most common approach. This may be further developed into full cross-fostering, where piglets are evened up for weight and distributed among sows according to their recorded performance or apparent milk output. Considerable improvements in mortality rates have been recorded – although piglets that have visibly loose droppings or are scouring should never be fostered.

Shift suckling or split-litter suckling is another technique which often suits the smaller herd with fewer chances of cross-fostering. This involves dividing a large litter into two equal weights of perhaps five big and seven smaller pigs. The five are placed in a crèche with water for about two feeds over one and a half to two hours; this allows the little ones to get feed and to take in extra quantities. It is not always necessary to remove them later because they will cope with missing a feed when the big pigs are there. Do this two to four times a day for about three days, and always within seven days of birth. Alternatively, in exceptionally large litters, do this with two groups of piglets until foster sows become available.

Back fostering is a technique where a small piglet is fostered on to a more recently farrowed sow. Do not do this if the piglet is scouring as it will get worse and could transfer disease. In larger herds where there are piglets being weaned twice a week, it is possible to step wean, where sows with bigger, stronger pigs are weaned a little early and the smaller weaker litters are kept back for a few days.

Split weaning is a more complicated version of step weaning. The piglets are not weaned until, as individuals, they are well over 5kg. Room is made on a litter not yet due to be weaned by weaning off the bigger pigs. This approach makes certain that sows are weaned on time.

Emergency fostering is sometimes necessary when the mother sow dies or becomes severely ill through disorders such as MMA. A nurse sow can be kept back after rearing her litter, and piglets from a sow one week off weaning moved on to her, a sow two weeks off on to hers, and the newly born on to the week-old litter's dam. It is complicated, but it only delays all of the sows' weaning by the equivalent of one sow's suckling period.

To have the equivalent of one nurse sow constantly would cost around £1,000 per annum; however, there are a number of piglet rearing systems available that use sow milk replacer, and these probably do the job more economically. In very large herds a more complicated version of using a nurse sow has been developed called 'restricted suckling'. Here, the rule is to restrict all sows to rear litters of, say, eleven piglets, based on previous performance.

The piglets from a sow that has suckled for fourteen days are moved into a crèche with either sow milk substitute or high quality solid feed. 'Rescue Decks' are a more recent option, where part or all of a litter can be reared on sow milk substitute. The same rules then apply as in the nurse sow approach. Do not forget to try to foster as soon after birth as possible, although modern sows are very good mothers and most will readily accept fostered piglets. Never foster sickly pigs. Make sure all foster piglets have a good opportunity to obtain colostrum (this should be achieved in two to three good sucks).

Piglets still struggling for a teat after twenty-four hours need help, and you will need to decide whether to foster them or their

Piglet crèche with sow milk substitute dispenser.

rival for a teat. Weaker piglets are usually better off on their own dam, so generally it is better to foster stronger piglets. Try and put foster piglets on to litters with smaller pigs than themselves. Remember that most piglets that die are starved in the first instance, even if the ultimate recorded cause of death is overlaying or scouring.

Supplementary Milk

Piglets reared in indoor maternity units can also be fed supplementary milk whilst suckling their dam. The British Denkavit 'Lifeline' product is supplied, in special drinkers, on an ad-lib basis from twelve hours after birth through to weaning, whilst the piglets continue to suckle their own mother. This will not replace the need for initial cross-fostering to even up litter sizes, but it could well reduce the need for fostering at a later stage.

Rescue decks and rescue cups are an example of some of the new developments designed to help rear the additional piglets produced by modern hyper-prolific breeding sows. Provimi introduced the systems in 2007, along with improved milk replacer formulas with modifications to prevent it going rancid or acidic.

Piglets can be reared away from, or close to the sow from one to three days of age until weaning in the fourth week of life. There is nothing new in this technology, and Heinrich Biehl had already developed a system for rearing piglets on acidified sow milk replacer in 1958. The Biehl system was developed to allow sows to be weaned at four days with the intention of getting the sows to farrow eleven piglets per litter 2.7 times per annum and so produce thirty weaned pigs per sow per year. The biological limits of the sow prevented this being achieved, but the piglets were fine and some claimed they were heavier and healthier at weaning age than those reared on the sow. Similar claims are now being made for piglets reared on these state-of-the-art milk replacer formulas.

Rescue decks and rescue cups are an example of some of the new developments designed to help rear the additional piglets produced by modern hyper-prolific breeding sows. Provimi introduced the systems in 2007, along with improved milk replacer formulas with modifications to prevent it going rancid or acidic. The piglets have a controlled microclimate and live in groups of about twelve piglets. The decks typically have three cups: one for water and two for milk. Milk is supplied via a pump from a storage bin.

Rescue deck with rescue cups. One of these is used to rear the weaker piglets from ten to twelve sows over a three-week period. The deck can be located high between two farrowing crates. The piglets can hear the sows and piglets during suckling.

There is a nipple in each cup, and this ensures a steady supply of milk without wastage.

There is also an option to have a full scale rescue-deck system in a nursery room away from the farrowing room, or to supply the milk via cups in the farrowing crates. The same milk mixing and preparation system and equipment is used.

It remains to be seen whether those herds rearing in excess of thirty pigs per sow per year will use a nurse sow or a combination of the technologies described above. Both approaches work, and the ultimate decision will be based on commercial success and acceptance of the systems on animal welfare and economic grounds. Reducing mortality rates in these hyperprolific pigs is a challenge even in the most productive modern breeding units. Well managed nurse sows and/or the application of advances in milk replacers and feeding/rearing systems will certainly play an ever-increasing role.

CREEP FEEDING

For many years we have been advised that offering creep feed to piglets from a few days old is desirable. When weaning was carried out before twenty-five days, pig farmers were split on the idea, with an equal number for and against creep feeding. Researchers at Bristol University highlighted the possibilities of an allergic response to the presence of certain types of protein, such as those in the soya bean products in creep feed. They found that post-weaning growth rates were poorer when such creep feeds were used, and that this was due to the piglet's immune system producing an antibody reaction to certain protein substances; these caused the villi (small finger-like projections lining the small intestine) to shorten, rather as they would during an *E. coli* attack, resulting in scours and poor feed conversion and growth. The problem is seen within four to five days of weaning, and the pig takes around fourteen days to recover partially. Specialist creeps have now been developed which avoid this problem in most instances, although other feed ingredients may produce similar effects – so it pays to take expert advice and use a creep feed that meets the needs of the piglets and the on-farm conditions.

The potential advantage of creep-fed piglets lies not so much with their very minor increase (if any) in weaning weight, but with the effect that early solid feed intake has on their digestive system. Enzymes are important in the digestion of food, and in the baby pig these chemical disintegrators are designed to digest milk. Very high quality (and high cost) baby piglet creep feeds will therefore contain milk products and very little starch from cereal grains. The digestive juices will change as new foods enter the system.

The graph demonstrates the X-factor principle. It shows how the milk-splitting enzymes are overtaken by the starch- and cereal-splitting enzymes, producing an X shape. It is suggested that creep-fed pre-weaning piglets will develop the ability to digest the less expensive cereal-based creeps more rapidly if they are fed creep. This should, in turn, result in faster and more economical growth rates after weaning. If piglets are weaned after twenty-five to twenty-eight days, then it is essential to provide creep feed because the sow will not provide enough feed through her milk, and the piglets will under-achieve.

If creep feeding is to be attempted from an early age, then begin to offer small quantities on a flat clean surface or container, replacing any that is uneaten at least twice a day. In most instances, seven to ten days after farrowing is often early enough to introduce creep. A traditional method was to use the 'frog' of a clean brick. Special creep hoppers are available, but do take care not to overfill them and let the feed get stale. Clever creep feeding involves a 'little and often' approach, with a maximum starting creep offering of just 20g (four heaped teaspoons) per litter per day.

Creep should be offered when piglets are active, and not just as they are waiting to suckle or are asleep. Always offer fresh creep at

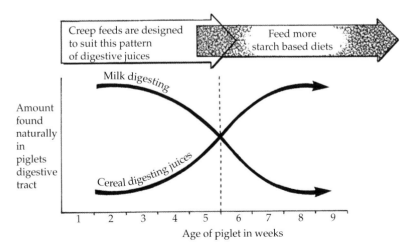

The 'X' factor.

least twice daily, and give the sow a treat by offering any remaining uneaten creep. Piglets will often eat no more than 100–200g by twenty-one to twenty-five days, although individual litters will consume many times that average. Remember that inadequate intake could lead to an immune response against protein. Outdoor herds weaning at up to twenty-five days or so have no trouble in getting piglets to take solid feed after weaning – in fact, outdoor piglets will often outgrow their indoor cousins who have had the benefit of creep feed. Our studies also showed they drink water more rapidly after weaning as compared to indoor-reared piglets.

MANAGEMENT OF THE WEANED PIG

Management of the weaned pig is not well defined, and the typical performance of the 'grower' section of many herds continues to demonstrate under-achievement. The potential for rapid efficient growth is there, but performance is affected by such factors as environment, nutrition, disease and possible lack of ambition in the stock person. Pigs weaned below four weeks of age have a number of problems: a poorly developed digestive system, a low ability to control body temperature, and a poorly developed immune system.

In nature, weaning is a gradual process complete at around twelve weeks, but at any age below eight weeks it puts demands on the stock person. At twenty-eight days of age we should be aiming for an average weaning weight of 8kg to ensure optimum growth through to slaughter weight.

Environment

The climatic environment is very important. Air temperature is a good measure, although you should take other factors such as pig weight, floor type (bedding), air speed (draughts) and feed level into account. These all influence heat production and loss in pigs. A 5kg pig needs to be around 8°C warmer than a 30kg one, and at three weeks of age, the temperatures required will be 29°C on perforated floors, and 27°C on straw-bedded floors or solid heated floors. (These drop to 21°C and 17°C respectively by 30kg.) Group size, insulation and radiant heat loss are also significant, and supplementary heating (often under-floor) is usually necessary.

Stocking density is also critical to performance, and all too often pigs are overcrowded for all the wrong reasons. Overcrowded pigs will keep warm and give off more heat huddled in a small area, but their appetite will be adversely affected and their growth rate reduced, whilst respiratory and digestive infections will increase. Slow-growing pigs are prone to the cold, and it is estimated that for every 100g growth reduction, the weaner's lower critical temperature will increase by about 1°C. The graph illustrates the amount of heat given off by a 5kg pig at different growth rates.

The fast-growing pig can be kept at a lower temperature. Although more heat input will be required at first in an environment of low stocking density, the pigs will grow faster, be more resistant to disease, and will move on faster to the next stage pens, making room for the next batch of pigs. A high of 26–28°C at pig level with no fast-moving air and a fresh atmosphere can only be managed at low stocking densities with ample heat input. This approach will allow a good appetite to develop.

Once growth rates rise, then supplementary heat can be reduced; one 5kg pig growing at 400g per day lets off more heat than two pigs growing at 50g per day. The slow grower needs to be kept wrapped up warm, whilst the fast grower needs to get rid of excess heat. It is, therefore, important to watch that the fast-growing pig can get rid of excess heat, or else appetite will suffer. A steady temperature reduction is as important as keeping up the initial temperature of the post-weaning house, because the appetite may reduce by 1g of

A 'two-climate' Trobridge mono-pitch weaner unit with a warm, solid-floored, lying and feeding area behind the plastic flaps and a cooler, comfortable, clean polymer cement slatted exercise and dunging area in the foreground. The warm zone is maintained by underfloor heating initially and then the piglets' own heat output, giving excellent energy efficiency. Temperature and ventilation is ACNV.

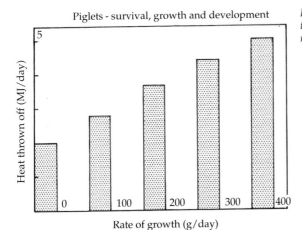

Piglets - survival, growth and development

Heat thrown off into the environment by a newly weaned 5kg pig.

feed for every 1°C of excess heat per kilogram of weaner pig body weight. So a 10kg pig kept at 10°C above the comfort zone will eat about 100g less each day. Therefore it is essential that the temperature is stepped down gradually from a maximum of 28°C at twenty-eight-day weaning to 18°C at the 30kg stage.

Nutrition

Firstly, water must be available and easily accessible to the weaned piglet. A piglet weaned at four weeks will dehydrate and lose body fat rapidly over the first forty-eight hours after weaning. Body fat reserves have been recorded as dropping from 15 to 7 per cent in the week following weaning. The use of cube drinkers or turkey drinkers with added sweeteners will help keep liquid intake up and help prevent digestive upsets and the development of post-weaning scours that are so often controlled unnecessarily with expensive and undesirable antibiotics.

Feed intake should be encouraged to the maximum, using an ad-lib or to-appetite approach, though it does take time to get pigs eating well after weaning. This is vital, as the first ten weeks of a piglet's life are those in which its food conversion is most efficient and growth most cost effective. The table gives suggested daily feed intakes and starting temperatures for piglets weaned at various weights (weight is more important than age in most instances).

Daily creep intake of individual piglets before weaning would be insignificant before and around ten days of age, rising to 10 to 30g daily between fourteen and twenty-one days, and around 60g per day during the fourth week of suckling. It must be borne in mind that

147

Live weight (kg)	Feed intake (g/day)	Perforated metal floors (°C)	Straw-bedded floors (°C)
5	126*	29	27
6	142*	29	27
	213**	27	25
7	157*	29	26
	235**	27	24

*probable intake **possible intake*

the day before weaning, a typical individual piglet will have consumed milk from its mother equivalent to about 300g of dry food. This exceptionally rich food would have the nutritional power of 500g a day of an expensive high-quality pre-starter pellet. In practice, after weaning at twenty-eight days, the piglet will eat about 10 per cent of this amount on the day following weaning. You can expect an initial intake of 100g of food per day, and you should increase this by about 40g per day until the pig weighs about 20kg. Size is more important than age, as big pigs will eat more and grow more quickly.

These figures underline the problems the pig faces: its diet is usually changed instantly from a warm, palatable liquid milk to a dry and less attractive pellet, crumb or meal at a time when its digestive and immune systems are immature and easily upset.

An example of a liquid-fed, 'two-climate' Trobridge weaner pen. The central liquid trough has automated yoghurt-based liquid feed delivery, and a temporary blue turkey drinker with gravity-fed water supply. The piglets are also initially offered piglet 'porridge' in the bowls after weaning. The lying area starts at 28°C and about 10 to 16°C or higher in the feeding, exercise and dunging area. The lying area has heated solid floors.

The food provided needs to be as close as possible in its composition to sow's milk (as far as ingredient costs will allow), and be of a highly digestible nature. Offer small quantities in the bottom of an ad-lib hopper or on a clean floor for the first few days, using the intakes suggested as a guide. It may be possible to feed some excellent diets ad lib from the first day, but in many instances, careful feeding will pay dividends. By the week after weaning, the thirty-five-day-old weaner should be eating 350g daily, and by fifty-six days and 20kg live weight, intake should be getting towards 1.2kg per day.

Professor Whittemore of Edinburgh University is often quoted as saying that 'it is every little pig's ambition to be a bigger pig'. Pigs do, indeed, have a formidable growth rate compared to other farm animals. The graph illustrates the typical growth rate of pigs from just before weaning through to thirty days after weaning. There are, however, a number of factors that can hinder the juvenile pig's growth rate, and you should ensure the following:

- Feed is kept fresh until eaten, and kept in short-term storage which is cool and dry
- Feed is left in hoppers for only a short time
- Feed contains the highest quality ingredients and is free from impurities, contaminants or anti-nutritional factors; the need for protein is high, but the quality and quantity fed must match the piglet and the farm circumstances
- The lysine content may be 1.4 per cent of the diet, or even higher. Even better than only looking at lysine, is to aim to provide an ideal protein profile that matches the needs of the weaner piglets. In other words, it should be high in quality protein and energy, have high palatability, and be readily eaten in large amounts

This suggests diets for piglets weaned during the fourth week of life that are highly digestible and which, therefore, do not contain too much vegetable protein or raw carbohydrate. A suitable and relatively simple pre-starter diet could be made up as follows:

Oat flakes (porridge)	38%
Dried skim milk	20%
Fat-filled milk	25%
Maize (corn) oil	10%
Glucose	5%
Minerals and vitamins	2%

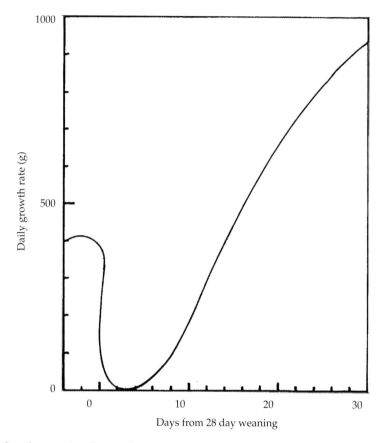

Growth expectation after weaning.

This would provide 17.5 MJ per kg of feed of digestible energy, 24 per cent crude protein, and 1.5 per cent lysine.

The pig producer now has a range of modern weaner diets available to match their situation. Expert advice is essential when choosing and evaluating if the chosen diet is achieving an optimum result.

An alternative to providing dry feed or a liquid feed is to use the 'Transition Feeder' that allows a smooth transition from sow's milk to dry or wet feed systems. The advantage of this approach is that it helps the piglets to move from regular hourly suckling to ad-lib feeding without causing digestive problems and scouring. It provides an instant mixing of feed, with fresh feed at each feeding and with adjustable time of feed. The water-to-meal ratio is adjustable, and a warm water version is available. These feeders can feed fifty piglets from as young as four days if necessary (with the appropriate milk replacer diet) through to 15kg. This is a little-and-often feeding system.

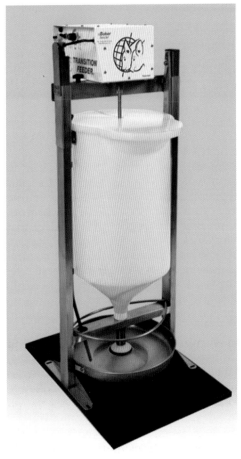

Baker 'Transition' feeder.

Controlled liquid mix feed delivery.

DISEASE

In order to reduce disease, you need to reduce stress. You can do this by providing clean, warm accommodation, handling the pigs quietly at all times, and keeping pig movements to the minimum. You should provide palatable creep at an early age (if practicable), reducing gut stress and producing a digestive pH (acidity) that prevents harmful (pathogenic) organisms from colonizing the gut. Dust, fumes and draughts should be reduced to protect the respiratory tract. Ensure that you provide good quality clean water in adequate, easily accessible quantities. If you get it right you can easily set yourself the target of a 30kg pig at nine to ten weeks for modern, improved pigs under commercial conditions.

Potential value of birth and weaning weights: Increased birth and weaning weights have a positive effect right through to finishing: 0.1kg heavier at birth = 0.2kg heavier at weaning, and 0.1kg heavier at weaning = one day less to reach slaughter weight. This will save approximately 1.8kg feed for each day saved. At £300 per tonne of feed, this is worth 54p for each day saved reaching slaughter weight. This means that a piglet 1kg heavier at weaning can potentially save about 18kg of finishing feed and cost £5.40 less to feed from weaning to slaughter weight.

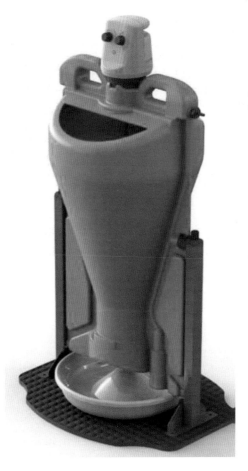

This 'Baker' feeder operates on a similar basis to the 'Transition Feeder', but is designed to feed up to forty-five piglets from weaning to 35kg.

This wet feeder also provides freshly mixed feed and is suitable for all feeds.

Hygiene is good, just like the 'Transition' model, with easy cleaning.

Feeding is controlled with variable feeding intervals through a simple electronic controller.

It is motor driven like the Transition Feeder, and also has variable rates of feed delivery.

7

The Finishing Pig

Once a pig reaches around 30kg you can begin to look at it in a very different way. You will be better equipped to predict how it will grow, and in fact can manipulate its carcase quality to fit the market at which you are aiming. There are several ways to feed a pig, ranging from diets based on liquid by-products to those based on cereals. Feeds can be wet or dry, meal or pellets, and can be delivered on the floor, in hoppers or troughs, completely automatically or by hand. So which approach should you adopt?

The ultimate choice must be based on sound economic principles and the type of raw materials available. Between 30kg and slaughter weight the pig is part of what is also known as the 'feeding herd', for very good reason, in that feed makes up about 75 per cent of the total cost of finishing pigs and around 80 per cent in the piglet from weaning to 30kg: making efficient use of feed must therefore always be the priority in the management of finishing pigs.

WET AND LIQUID FEEDING

Wet feed is usually efficient in terms of feed conversion and good feed intakes; however, it is important to get the mixture to the right consistency (of porridge, not soup). Use a water-to-meal ratio of 2.5:1 and avoid higher dilutions, otherwise the pig will be unable to consume enough and growth rate will be below expectation. Wet feed is more difficult to ration correctly than dry feed, and it is important to avoid wastage.

Good hygiene is absolutely essential in pipeline wet-feed systems. Keep a close eye on the pigs' appetite, and check the frequency and accuracy of feeding. Pigs usually satisfy their appetite in about twenty minutes twice a day when trough or floor feeding a rationed or restricted diet. Automatic systems now provide a very accurate metering of feed, both wet and dry, and although the capital costs are high, when managed correctly, the returns on investment are excellent.

MEAL OR PELLETS?

Research work at the Hillsborough Research Institute in Northern Ireland showed that with ad-lib feeding, feed conversion is 7.6 per cent worse with meal than with pellets. In other words, it takes more to feed a bacon pig on meal than it does with pellets. This is due to the higher levels of wastage and spillage measured. Respiratory problems such as enzootic pneumonia and atrophic rhinitis tend to be aggravated by meal dust, which leads to lower feed intakes. Pelleting will add up to 3 per cent to the cost of a finishing diet, but where meal cannot be fed wet or using a mix-at-the-trough feeder, it repays this several times over.

FLOOR, TROUGH OR HOPPERS?

The most inefficient way to feed fatteners is to throw meal on the floor. You should always use pellets if floor feeding, or if you have to feed meal on the floor, moisten it first to reduce wastage. If at all possible, you should feed meal in a trough or specially designed feeder. It is a good idea to add about 4.5ltr of water to 3kg of meal in a trough when feeding manually.

Avoiding wastage is an important rule, and one which applies to all systems of feeding. Ad-lib hoppers must be checked frequently to ensure that there is a free flow without excess feed being available for the pigs to root out on to the floor. Most ad-lib hoppers have some form of adjustment helping to control the flow of feed.

Feed Availability in a Trough Feeder

Pig weight (kg)	Trough/hopper length (mm)/ pig for restricted feeding	Trough/hopper length (mm)/ pig for ad-lib feeding
5	100	75
10	130	33
15	150	38
35	200	50
60	240	60
90	280	70
120	300	75

Source: Dr John Carr, Murdoch University, Australia (*The Pig Journal Proceedings Supplement 1*, April 2008).

'Mix-at-the-trough' feed delivery systems have gained in popularity. These vary from what appear to be narrow or single-space feeders, resembling ad-lib hoppers, with water drinkers attached, through to round trough (Turbomat/Blu'Hox type) feeders. The hopper types usually provide feed at all times. The pigs root a plate or move a bar lever to earn food, which can be eaten dry or usually mixed with water by depressing the drinker and mixing it. These feeders seem to achieve good feed intakes and to reduce feed wastage considerably; however, it is important to monitor the effect of various approaches to feeding on carcase grading performance and the price achieved.

The table on page 155 illustrates why full-length dry feed hoppers work well for piglets immediately after weaning. When fed ad lib, the newly weaned pig needs a ten times greater restricted feed trough width, and more than twenty times the width in relation to its size than a 120kg pig. This underlines the importance of providing the weaned piglet with the optimum trough space in order to ensure subsequent top level finishing pig performance.

This table illustrates a typical 10 per cent loss of feed compared to the theoretical 0 per cent loss. The total wastage between four weeks and twenty-two weeks of age is likely to be 20 to 25kg of feed. This would add between £6 and £7.50 to the feed costs per pig (2013) prices, or 60P to 75p per 1 per cent increase. The table also illustrates how feed intake and growth rate increase over time, and how FCR (FCE) deteriorates as pigs grow heavier. The FCR values are spot calculation at each of the specified live weights.

The Effect of Actual Feed Usage at a Typical 10% Wastage Level

Age (weeks)	Gain (g/day)	FCR (0% loss)	Feed intake (kg/day)	FCR (10% loss)	Feed use (kg) 10% waste
4	215	1:1	0.215	1.1:1	0.237
6	395	1.2:1	0.474	1.32:1	0.521
8	630	1.4:1	0.882	1.54:1	0.970
10	660	1.6:1	1.056	1.76:1	1.162
12	715	1.8:1	1.287	1.98:1	1.416
14	800	2.4:1	1.920	2.64:1	2.112
16	965	2.6:1	2.509	2.86:1	2.760
18	1,000	2.9:1	2.900	3.19:1	3.190
20	1,100	3.0:1	3.300	3.30:1	3.630
22	1,100	3.2:1	3.520	3.52:1	3.872

Adapted from: Dr John Carr, Murdoch University, Australia (*The Pig Journal Proceedings Supplement 1*, April 2008).

Performance Levels in UK Finishing Pigs (30–100kg)

	Potential	Good	Average	Poor
Feed intake (kg/day)	2.06	2.16	2.0	1.9
Gain (g/day)	1250	900	700	600
FCR (feed to gain)	1.65:1	2.3:1	2.8:1	3.0:1
P2 (mm) backfat	7.5	10.0	10.5	12.0
Feed cost saving (£/pig)	20	10	3	0
Feed fed per pig (kg)	115.5	161	196	210

Adapted from: BPEX KTB 18 *Feeding Health Challenge,* 2013.

These figures are based on modern improved pigs and cannot be applied directly to traditional or unimproved strains of pig.

GROWTH AND CARCASE PERFORMANCE

Manipulating growth and carcase performance is relatively easy with the modern high-performance hybrid; however, it can be easy to produce too much fat with some rare breeds and strains of outdoor pig. The question that must be answered is, should you go for maximum growth, or maximum lean meat and an absence of excess fat? In a perfect world, these would be one and the same thing, and this may well be the case with some modern pigs on tailor-made diets. Much depends on the pig.

Managing the finishing pig should not be seen as a second-rate skill in pig production. A one per cent improvement in the feed efficiency of finishing pigs would be worth around £0.75; assuming twenty-four pigs sold per sow, it is worth £18 per sow per year in 2013. Thus a typical 500 sow herd rearing pigs from birth to slaughter would be saving £9,000 per annum for each 1 per cent improvement in feed conversion efficiency (FCE).

The task is to maximize lean meat growth at a cost directly related to the financial return from the market-place. The first point to be aware of is the fact that we have potentially three sexes of pig with differing nutritional requirements and growth and carcase characteristics. The entire male pig converts feed more efficiently than his sister, and they both convert more efficiently than their castrated brother. The reason for this is simple: the entire male benefits from male hormones that stimulate the growth and development of lean meat (the anabolic effect). The castrated male grows less lean meat each day and deposits more fat. Lean meat requires just over 1kg of feed to produce a 1kg gain, compared to fat, which requires in excess of 4kg to produce the deposition of 1kg. Fat is no longer desired by the consumer in the quantities formerly grown, and it is expensive to produce.

The amount of potential daily lean tissue growth in entire and castrated pigs of between 20 and 90kg live weight, and of a traditional genotype, would typically be as follows:

	Entire	
	Males	Castrates
Food conversion ratio	2.6:1	3.0:1
Lean tissue growth/day (g)	280	230

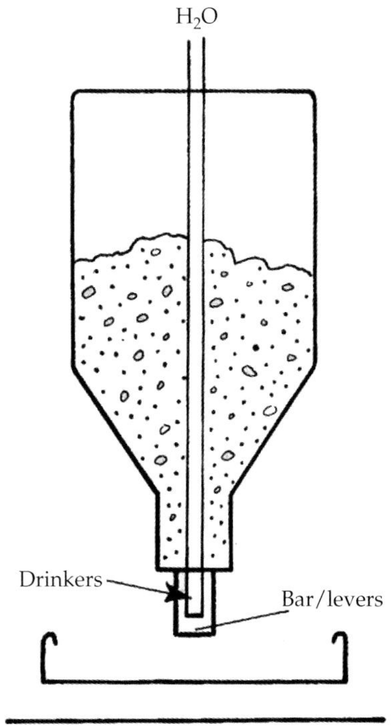

Displacement bar principle
(several variants)

Midway in price
Popular in America
Pigs feed both sides

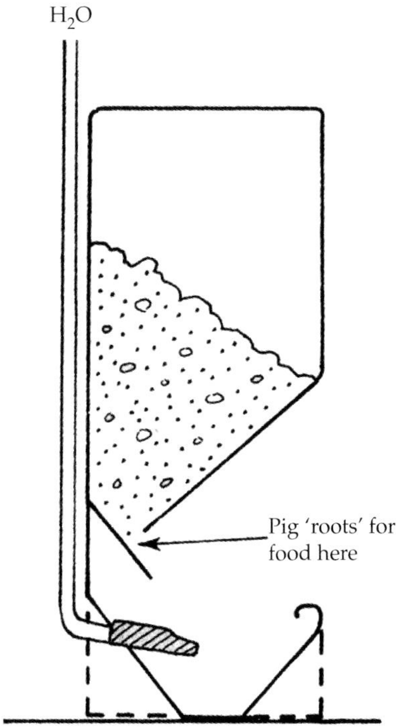

Rooting principle
Cheap
Some models tend
to block
Popular in Europe
One pig feeds at a time

Above and opposite: Three very different mix-at-the-trough delivery systems. JOHN GADD

Twin single space 'mix-at-the-trough' feeders fitted to supply two Trobridge pens. This also illustrates the computer-controlled, rear inlet ventilation flaps. The width of the slat gap is also now defined as a legal maximum (EU), and must be modified or replaced if it does not conform.

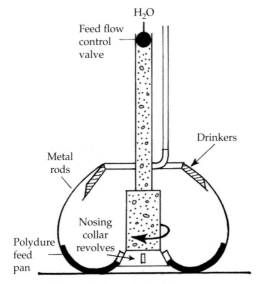

H_2O

Feed flow control valve

Drinkers

Metal rods

Nosing collar revolves

Polydure feed pan

Rotary (turbomat) principle
Computerized
Timed eating and drinking
Expensive in capital
Popular in Europe
10 feed places in circle
Polydure feed pan (silicon quartz)

Three very different mix-at-the-trough delivery systems. JOHN GADD

159

This version illustrates a two pen shared, double width, full length liquid feed trough. The internal baffle is adjustable to create a warmer lying area at the rear. The pigs dung and urinate in the cooler, front part of the monopitch pen. The slotted areas in the slat panels are increased in the dunging area.

A pig's eye view from the pen on to a parallel row of Trobridge monopitch weaner pens. The rack-and-pinion drive for the rear flaps, feed/inspection flap and front flap motor housing can be seen, along with the manual internal flap winch on the centre pillar. This fully open front flap illustrates how the ACNV system allows excellent ventilation and high air exchange rates.

Straw-based Trobridge pens with solid internal floors with bedding. Mucking out is achieved by scraping through the dunging area using a tractor with all the swing gates closed. These are high welfare organic pigs. ACNV is also fitted.

These values are for unimproved pigs in 2013, but illustrate the difference caused by the entire pig's anabolic (hormone) effect. Improved pig strains can easily grow 500g of lean per day. Genetic selection continues to improve this key performance factor even further, with some new hybrid lines claiming a 2.5 per cent improvement in feed efficiency over their recent predecessors. Using the data from our example above, this would translate into a £23,500 improvement per annum in the 500 sow herd example.

There may also be an improvement in carcase quality, and this will provide a potential additional financial improvement through higher carcase prices. The gilt would perform somewhere between the two types of male for these growth and performance characteristics. In modern white breeds and their crosses, there is no reason to treat the sexes differently up until about 50kg live weight.

With pigs above 50kg live weight, sex differences are considerable and split-sex feeding may well be profitable, certainly in the larger unit. From a nutritional point of view and in order to express lean tissue growth to the full, the entire male needs about 10 per cent more lysine each day than the female, and she, in turn, requires about 10 per cent more than the castrate (or hog) pig.

It is unlikely that you will finish both entire and castrated pigs on the same unit, but if you do, it will be essential to split-sex feed them, not only because of the difference in lysine requirements, but also because the hog pig will produce a fatter carcase. If you feed entires, gilts and castrates on the same diet and feed scale, then you would need to slaughter them at different weights to keep the same back-fat level.

PRACTICAL FEEDING

The question most difficult to answer is: should you be feeding ad lib all the way to slaughter, or feeding ad lib up to 40 or 50kg live weight and then to a scale designed to optimize the cost of producing the carcase and obtaining the best possible return from the market-place? The latter is probably the correct approach for many pig producers, unless their pigs are bred for ad lib finishing. The following table illustrates a very typical traditional scale-feeding approach from around 20 to 90kg live weight.

Feed scales are usually related to pig weight, but also sometimes to pig age. The pig's appetite is related to its live weight, and weight is probably the best basis for fixing the ration. Many people feed pigs to appetite until a certain intake is achieved and keep to a scale from then on. These feed scales are a guide only, but adjustments

Daily Feed Allowance (Medium Energy Diet)

Age (wks)	Weight (kg)	Improved strains and entire males (kg/day)	Gilts (kg/day)	Castrates (kg/day)
9	21	1.00	1.00	1.00
11	27	1.35	1.35	1.35
13	35	1.75	1.60	1.50
15	46	2.05	1.80	1.62
17	58	2.20	1.95	1.74
19	70	2.35	2.05	1.85
21	80	2.45	2.15	1.94
23	90	2.55	2.25	2.02
25	99	2.65	2.35	2.11

will be necessary to suit each given set of circumstances, such as a higher or lower nutrient density. Modern hybrid pigs will also require a different feed scale and diet specification compared to the traditional breeds, and especially those that are early maturing and finish at lighter weights. An example is that a modern 60kg pig growing at 800g per day will require 9.5 MJ/day for maintenance, 5.7 MJ/day for protein growth (130g/day) and 10.2 MJ/day for fat growth (190g/day). This adds up to 25.4 MJ/day in 2kg feed, giving an FCR of 2.5:1.

The weights given in the 'Daily Feed Allowance' example are on an as-fed dry matter basis and will need to be adjusted for wet feeding: this is normally done by adding water at 2.5 to 1. If liquid milk or other liquid by-products are used, it will be necessary to take advice in both formulating the ration and calculating the volumes to feed, although they should be around two and a half times the values given above in most instances.

Ad-Lib Feeding

This is simply defined as the feeding of animals by any method where they have close to a twenty-four-hour unrestricted access to feed. Ad-lib hoppers and mix-at-the-trough single-space feeders do this in slightly different ways. There is no doubt that once weaner pigs can take it, they should be ad-lib fed through to 40 or 50kg – indeed it is difficult, if not impossible, to overfeed a modern pig below this weight. The approach adopted above this weight will depend in large measure on the diet specification, the pig, and the method of feeding.

Grower diet (£/t)	315
Finisher diet (£/t)	277
Weight at entry (kg)	30
Transfer weight (kg)	60
Slaughter weight (kg)	100
Grower feed (kg/pig)	59
Finisher feed (kg/pig)	136
Total feed (kg/pig)	194
FCR Growing stage	1.96
FCR Finishing stage	3.39
FCR Overall	2.78
P2 (mm)	11.0
Carcass weight (kg)	76.0

FCR Adjuster	-2%	▲ ▼

Enter figures in the yellow boxes
Change FCR using the adjuster

Feed cost of last kg live weight gained (p/kg dead weight)	152.43

Cost of production (£/pig)		£
Weaner costs (£)		45.00
Feeding Herd Only		
Feed		
	Grower	18.55
	Finisher	37.54
	Overall	56.10
Veterinary & Med		0.76
Transport & Marketing		3.30
Electricity & Gas		0.51
Water		0.40
Straw & bedding		0.80
Other variable costs		0.37
Labour (including family)		3.80
Building depreciation		4.22
Building repairs & maintenance		0.10
Equipment depreciation		0.48
Equipment repairs & maintenance		0.05
Other fixed costs		1.12
TOTAL COSTS (£/pig)		117.01
TOTAL COSTS (p/kg Dead Weight)		153.95
Average Sale value (£/pig)		117.04
Average Sale value (p/kg Carcass)		154.00

Net Margin		
	(p/kg Dead Weight)	0.05
	(£/pig)	0.04

The BPEX calculator service: available online to allow pig farmers to assess online their performance and the effects of changes in prices/costs and a percentage change in feed conversion ratio. It also provides a useful overview of the costs involved in producing a finishing pig. This example shows a result close to breaking even in the summer of 2013.

It also assists the producer in determining that the slaughter weight chosen (100kg) is close to the economic maximum in this case because each 1kg increase in carcase weight is already costing 152.3p, and the average sale price is only 154p.

Available at: www.bpex.org.uk/publications/2TS/calculators.asp.

Most pigs (apart from low-appetite strains) should be fed a little less than their appetite calls for, in order to prevent them from laying down too much fat at significantly increased feeding costs. Research (Kanis, 1988) suggests that the optimum feed conversion of lean meat tissue is achieved at 86 per cent of ad-lib intake, although it was also found that castrated males were at their most efficient at 75 per cent of ad-lib intake. As pigs have improved, we have been able to exploit some genotypes ad lib through to slaughter, and these figures have certainly changed. Ad lib is already a sensible approach if pigs are slaughtered at 60kg to 80kg live weight, and with careful diet formulation and management, some of the improved strains will be capable of growing lean meat efficiently well beyond this weight.

Ad-lib feeding traditionally had a place in most finishing units in countries such as the USA, where excess fat was removed after slaughter and flat rate payments are made regardless of lean meat content. Times change, however, and carcase quality is now a universal goal. Ad-lib fed pigs also have an advantage in killing out percentage which can easily be 1 to 2 per cent better than pigs fed on extremely restricted diets.

OPTIMUM SLAUGHTER WEIGHTS AND CARCASE GRADING

Weighing pigs prior to slaughter will pay dividends in payment schedules with tight weight ranges. You should keep accurate records of weights sent and have them analysed by computer in order to find the optimum sale weight – overweight and underweight pigs can cost money. Do not forget that heavier pigs will have more back fat than lighter pigs. Pigs are normally graded based on the carcase weight and back fat thickness in millimetres (mm) at the P2, and/or their lean meat content when more sophisticated measuring devices are used. The aim is to get as many pigs as economically as possible into the top grade(s) and payment contract box.

Pig unit managers should be able to determine the following from a good carcase grading evaluation programme:

- Define the optimum weight and spread of weights to aim for to achieve an optimum carcase sale value
- Define the optimum P2 mm or lean meat percentage and range to aim for at the optimum weight, as defined above
- Predict the change effected in P2 or lean meat percentage when it is advised to increase or decrease carcase weight, provide a reliable grading forecast, and predict price per kg carcase
- It is also desirable to be able to simulate the 'sale' of the herd's pigs into another contract or change in contract specification using the current weight, weight spread and P2/lean percentage values

Profitable Slaughter Pig Selection

The following graphs illustrate two sets of slaughter pig data analysed to examine how well they were rewarded from the same pig carcase grading contract.

Getting as many pigs as possible into the correct weight and P2 fat depth range (or ranges) brings a significant financial reward. Each blue diamond represents pigs that were sold at the corresponding

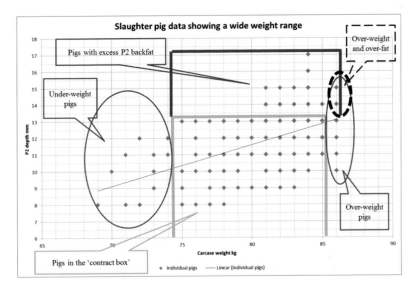

Chart 1: This chart contains pigs that were sold at too wide a weight range. This resulted in pigs being sold underweight and overweight, and these failed to fit into the 'contract box' where the best prices per kg carcase are achieved.

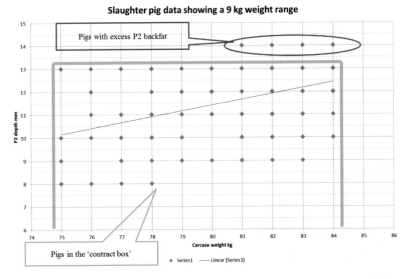

Chart 2: This shows a much better picture, with only a small number of pigs 'downgraded' because they had too much P2 back fat depth.

weight and back fat. Chart 1 had eleven pigs sold too light and thirteen too heavy, and these were paid for at a reduced rate per kg. Two of the thirteen over-weight pigs were also over-fat and had further reductions in price. The remaining fifty-one pigs were in the contract box where the best prices are paid. In this batch of pigs, only two-thirds of the pigs were on target, and one-third were not.

Chart 2 illustrates a batch of pigs that all fitted into the 'contract box' by weight, and only four were downgraded for a 1mm excess in P2 back-fat measurement. Lean meat percentage values based on more sophisticated carcase grading systems can also be analysed using similar methods.

The trend lines show how back fat increases with live weight. Chart 1 has pigs that are getting fatter more rapidly as they increase in weight than those in Chart 2.

These two sets of data illustrate why regular computer analysis of pig slaughter information can help make decisions to achieve the best, or better said, optimum prices. Too many producers lose out at this last hurdle and are penalized financially for doing so.

More and more pig producers are now having their slaughter pig data analysed, but these procedures are not in universal use in 2013, despite the methodology and technology having been available in various forms for approaching thirty years.

- Chart 1 and Chart 2: Derived from Beynon, N. M. 'Pig Marketing – evaluation of graded market outlets for slaughter pigs using micro-processor based statistical models'. CGLI Insignia Award in Technology Thesis, August 1985.

WEIGHING METHODS

Most pigs are either weighed individually and also as a group. Accurate weighing provides accurate growth rate data and ensures that a batch of pigs is marketed as close as possible to the 'ideal' slaughter weight. For small-scale producers a weigh band is available to estimate live weight based on the distance round a specific band around the animal's trunk. A hand-held video image analysis device is also available that can be used to estimate pig weight within a reasonable degree of error.

Recent developments include the fitting of automatic electronic weighing devices into large group finishing pen systems. Other versions also include the facility to direct the individual pigs to a specific feeding pen to control the amount and type of feed offered, as well as selecting pigs above a certain weight for sale by drafting them into a collection pen. Growth rates can be monitored and pigs automatically marked and even sorted for sale.

It is interesting to note that these systems frequently show that the finishing pigs are not growing well during the last stage prior to slaughter. This provides good evidence that many finishing pigs actually slow down during the last few weeks. This is probably due to factors such as inadequate feed intake caused by a lack of space or trough access for these heavier pigs. Entire male pigs can also become increasingly restless and aggressive as they get older and heavier. Pigs are also sometimes mixed after the larger pen mates are removed, resulting in fighting and aggression. Weighing pigs should not be confined only to recording the individual pig's weight at entry and prior to sale.

The table below lists the 'top six' key performance indicators for finishing pigs, and shows that a pig in a herd achieving average performance costs nearly £12 more to feed than a pig in a top 10 per cent herd. Feed cost per tonne is a significant factor along with feed conversion efficiency. The top 10 per cent have a feed cost nearly 20 per cent lower than the average, combined with a feed conversion efficiency nearly 15 per cent better than the average producer. This is probably being achieved through the sourcing and use of high quality economical by-product and co-product feeds on a large scale, combined with top class advice and monitoring by a nutritionist and consultant veterinarian.

Finishing pig housing and accommodation in the UK continues to be an area of concern in 2013. Considerable investment is required to ensure that UK pig producers can compete economically with other importing countries in Europe and beyond.

Finishing Pig Performance (between 35kg and 110kg live weight)

12 months to June, 2013	Top 10%	Top third	Average
Weight of pig produced (kg)	105.8	104.11	100.39
Mortality (%)	2.76	2.65	2.88
Feed conversion ratio	2.4:1	2.61:1	2.81:1
Daily live-weight gain (g/day)	918	851	800
Feed cost per tonne (£)	210.03	219.93	259.09
Feed cost per pig produced (£)	31.24	36.90	43.02

Source: BPEX 09/2013
www.bpex.org/prices-facts-figures/costings/KPIFinishing.aspx

Feeding the finishing pig is a skilled job, so do take plenty of advice and keep adequate records based on the environment and health of your pigs, financial and feed inputs, sale output and carcase grading information. Efficient and effective finishing pig management is worth many thousands of pounds per annum in the most modest-sized pig unit.

www.thepigsite.com/pigjournal/articles/2169/management-practices-to-reduce-expensive-feed-wastage.

8

Sow and Gilt Management

The management of sows and gilts has developed in line with the breeding of quick-growing lean pigs, along with an increase in the number of pigs born and reared per sow per year, and of course, improved scientific knowledge and understanding. The more recent development of hyper-prolific breeding sows has continued to challenge preconceptions about gilt and sow management.

Gilt management will depend on whether they are reared from selection or purchased at around 60kg, or brought into the herd only six to ten weeks prior to first mating. Special diets are recommended for rearing gilts from 60kg to mating. Modern hybrid gilts are exceptionally lean animals, growing to 100kg at least fifty to sixty days faster than their forebears. Do not mate modern hybrid gilts before 130 to 140kg live weight or 230 to 240 days of age. Aim for their second or third oestrus at first service or insemination.

Grow gilts a little more slowly to achieve, by first mating, the 18mm P2 minimum back-fat cover more easily accomplished at this slightly older and heavier stage than that of the traditional breeds. Gilt selection or purchase at around 100kg at 160 to 170 days of age will ensure that they have at least four weeks isolation and a further six to eight weeks before they are ready for pregnancy. This provides sufficient time for quarantine and for the gilts to acclimatize to the farm and develop some resistance to the resident pathogens before joining the main herd.

Flushing by feeding a higher daily ration for two weeks prior to mating can produce up to two more eggs, especially when gilts are served too light, too young, and/or too thin. Do not overfeed during the first pregnancy, and always reduce gilt feed intakes immediately after they are mated or inseminated to help embryo survival. Take it steadily, and aim for 20 to 24mm P2 back fat at farrowing.

You will also need to get your lactation feeding intakes high. The same target applies to sows at weaning. Gilts can regularly make up 20 per cent of the breeding herd entering the farrowing house at any one time. Specialist gestation and lactation diets are available for gilts and even second litter sows, or sows with poor appetites and those with very large litters.

Lactation feeding is one of the most critical areas of sow and gilt feeding management. The major indicator for you to keep a watchful eye on at this stage is appetite. You can control lactation appetite with clever feeding, but this begins before farrowing and it is influenced by a number of factors.

NUTRITIONAL NEEDS OF THE SOW AND GILT

Sow feeding can be divided into three phases: lactation, weaning to service, and gestation. A large sow with a large litter could easily require 90–100MJ of DE per day if you are aiming to keep back-fat losses down. A lactation diet would typically contain 13.5MJ of DE per kilogram of feed. Taking 100MJ of DE as her daily requirement, simple mathematics calculates the daily feed intake target as 7.4kg. Many herds find difficulty in exceeding 5 or 6kg at the most, and their sows have to find around 30MJ a day from their own body reserves. Scientists estimate that 1kg of net body-fat loss in the sow during lactation will produce about 38MJ. This suggests that a sow with a shortfall of 30MJ of DE a day will lose about 0.75kg of body fat each day. Over twenty-eight days, this would add up to more than 22kg of body fat alone. Muscle weight loss yields less energy than fat and would result in even greater weight loss.

This fat loss figure is well in excess of the 10 to 15kg maximum recommended, but it is often exceeded. If a sow or, even worse, a gilt exceeds this level of loss, she could be in a 'nose dive' too steep to pull out from. This is likely to happen when 50MJ of DE or less per day is taken in during lactation (the equivalent of about 3.5kg of feed per day). In short, you cannot provide the sow with too much energy during lactation. It is interesting to note that the 'Nottingham System' of estimating the required ration for lactating sows was based on 1.8kg for the sow and 0.5kg for each piglet, giving a maximum of 7.8kg for a sow with twelve piglets suckling. This was coupled with advice to feed 2kg on the day of farrowing and increasing to the maximum by feeding 0.5kg extra per day until the maximum is achieved. Feeding two to three times per day is recommended to keep the appetite sharp.

Two-Diet Sow Feeding

The gestating sow and the lactating sow and gilt will benefit tremendously from the use of at least two specific diet formulations.

170

Examples of Two-Diet Feeding

Diets	Protein (%)	Oil (%)	Fibre (%)	Lysine (%)	DE(MJ)
Standard sow feed	13.00	3.5	5.05	0.60	12.49
Lactation sow feed	18.00	6.67	5.05	0.95	13.80

Two-diet feeding involves a low-protein pregnancy diet followed by a high-protein and lysine lactation diet with an appropriate energy, micro-nutrient balance. The advantage seems to come from the sows putting down less protein (excess protein is expensive to grow), and conserving more fat during pregnancy, which, in turn, is more useful to them during lactation. It is suggested that appetite during lactation is also improved. Sows fed on this two-diet system are lighter by about 15 to 20kg at the fourth parity (litter) and require less feed to maintain body processes than those fed a single diet throughout.

It is recommended that you increase feed levels from about day ninety of pregnancy in order to provide for the rapidly developing piglets. Feeding lactation diets prior to farrowing is often recommended because they contain a special cocktail of essential fatty acids that help boost sow milk output and piglet energy reserves. Higher lysine in lactation diets also boosts milk output, and where lactating sow feed intakes are low, there is a benefit from feeding a diet with up to 1.2 per cent lysine and 15 MJ DE. This is useful during very hot weather.

SUCKLING SOW FEEDING ADVICE

Lactation feeding is one of the most critical areas of sow and gilt feeding management. The major indicator to keep a watchful eye on at this stage is appetite. You can control lactation appetite with clever feeding, but this begins before farrowing and it is influenced by a number of factors.

Do not forget that there are significant differences in feed intake or appetite (plus or minus several kilograms per day) between breeds and the various crosses and specialized hybrids. Obtain expert practical advice from nutritionists and your breeding stock supplier.

Overfeeding sows during pregnancy to make up for a serious weight loss during lactation is a classic syndrome. This can result in excessive weight loss in the next lactation, and so on throughout its productive life. If you are going to feed more to improve condition during pregnancy, you need to do so during the first half of pregnancy. This means starting early. If thin sows are fattened up in late pregnancy – for example, over 45MJ of DE per day for more than twenty days – this can lead to 0.5 to 1kg less feed eaten in each day of lactation. Condition score your sows, and aim for a minimum of 2.5 at weaning and 3.5 at farrowing.

Temperatures over 21°C in the farrowing house reduce appetite. According to work carried out by pig consultant John Gadd, CO_2 levels below 0.3 per cent in a farrowing house kept at 22 to 23°C produced no depression in appetite. However, it was found that reductions of up to 2kg per day were experienced when CO_2 exceeded 0.5 per cent at 22 to 23°C. Slightly improved ventilation and a drop to 21°C caused the appetite to return to normal, with the same CO_2 level. This suggests that both temperature and air freshness/ventilation are very important for housed lactating sows.

Outdoor farrowing arcs can also get extremely hot in summer, and it might be a good idea to insulate or whitewash these. Wallows and shade are essential for both dry and lactating sows during hot spells.

Water is closely linked to appetite in all classes of pig, and sows are no exception, particularly during lactation, when they could be producing in excess of 15ltr of milk each day at peak yield. Foods vary tremendously in their thirst-making properties and you should check flow rates. Remember that a sow can drink up to 30ltr a day.

Method of feeding is very important. Just prior to farrowing, and immediately afterwards, sows and gilts will often suffer from a depressed appetite. Too much 'rich' food at this time can upset milk quality and the udder, where the milk is made. However, it is equally wrong to 'starve' the sow or gilt at this time in order to prevent MMA syndrome (mastitis metritis agalactia), or nutritional 'looseness' (scours) in the very young piglet.

The skill to develop is one that keeps the appetite sharp. With some feeds it is useful to mix in about 0.25 to 0.5kg of bran per day, although correctly fed modern lactation diets should not pose this problem. By about the fourth day after farrowing you should then remove the bran and try to increase the feed intake towards the maximum, if the sow can take it. Be patient – it can take up to ten or twelve days in individual cases: remember that sows are individuals and not machines.

The 'Stotfold' feed scale has achieved considerable improvements in intake for many herds and is based on the principle of working with, and adjusting intake according to the appetite, age, size, and litter size of the individual sow or gilt. Liquid feeds can also follow a similar feed scale, suitably converted to the wet mix volume or weight. (An example 'Stotfold' scale recording sheet is included in Appendix I.)

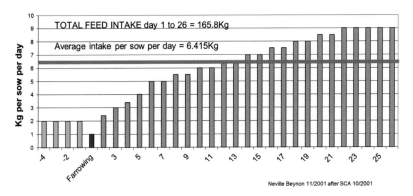

Stotfold scale lactation feed intake example: the average for sows and gilts is 13.5MJ/kg, 17 per cent crude protein and 0.95 per cent lysine, where herd production averages twenty-six piglets per sow per year (10/2001). NEVILLE BEYNON 11/2001 AFTER SCA 10/2001

It is important to make every effort to avoid overfeeding energy during embryo attachment or implantation, which lasts from around day nine to day seventeen post mating. Current advice suggests that most damage occurs while the embryos are attaching to the wall of the womb when energy/feed intake exceeds 38MJ of DE, or 3kg of feed per day. This rule certainly applies to gilts. Gilts should be mated in good condition, and this problem should not arise. If it does, avoid overfeeding gilts to improve body condition during at least the first month of gestation. The 3kg limit for sows allows you to increase feed for sows in low condition immediately post weaning, and improve body condition to the desired level during the first half of pregnancy when the conceptus requires relatively low levels of nutrients, because the uterus, placenta and foetuses are growing slowly.

Keeping the feed intake high (flushing) from weaning to first service is considered good practice as it can help increase litter sizes. Feeding the higher nutrient density lactation diet for the five days until oestrus begins may also be beneficial, and will not add much to the total feed costs.

There is also a strong argument in favour of increasing sow feed intake from around day ninety of gestation to meet the increased demand for nutrients by the rapidly growing foetuses. This increased feed level can be maintained until two or three days before farrowing. Take expert advice that matches your sow's needs and farm situation.

SEASONAL (SUMMER AND AUTUMN) INFERTILITY

The pig is best described as an opportunistic breeder. The European wild boar (*Sus scrofa*) usually gives birth in spring, but exactly when this occurs is very much controlled by the availability of sufficient feed during the previous summer/autumn. The wild boar sow will often farrow in January in central Europe where the previous summer allowed for an early increase in feed intake that stimulates oestrus and mating in early autumn. However, weather conditions are frequently exceptionally cold in January, and the whole litter can be lost. When this happens, these sows will usually come into oestrus again very rapidly and conceive to farrow again in late spring.

Our modern domestic pig exhibits some seasonal fertility patterns that are often present more severely on one farm compared to another. It can be managed to a large extent by good nutritional and environmental management. Sows can also come into oestrus during lactation, especially where nutrient intakes during lactation are very high; this is particularly likely when they are in good condition or multi-suckling in groups, for example outdoors. The timing of these oestrus events can easily span from the first week to the fifth week of lactation; this explains why some sows do not come into oestrus for two to three weeks after weaning.

Consistent findings from studies into seasonal infertility point to sudden and rapid increases in environmental temperatures as the common factor related to a subsequent decline in fertility. In one case it was found that a sudden increase from unusually very cold spring temperatures to a high of only 19°C caused a significant drop in fertility on an outdoor unit in the UK during April 2013.

Sugar-beet pulp is an excellent feed ingredient, and it can also help generate useful additional body heat for breeding pigs during cold winter months as compared to oils and fats. However, this could lead to problems during very hot spells, and it may be wise to use fats and oils to provide the energy source in both gestation and lactation diets during the summer months. Higher nutrient density lactation and less bulky diets may also be useful during hot periods when lactating sow appetites are reduced.

The pig unit manager can sensibly view seasonal infertility as a sudden temperature shock-related management syndrome. All practical measures to reduce its potential impact should be implemented, based on sound advice. This must be directly relevant to the specific conditions present on the individual pig unit, and may involve using wallows and shades outdoors, or better ventilation and water sprinklers or misters indoors. Planned increases in the number of gilts brought in, and culling fewer sows, can help maintain piglet production where the problem occurs regularly.

WEIGHT, BACK-FAT THICKNESS AND BODY CONDITION SCORES

Used together, these three measurements can provide an excellent basis for monitoring the nutritional management of sows and gilts. Condition scores – from 1: very thin, to 5: over fat – are very useful indicators of how close the sow is to the body condition considered ideal at various stages in her production cycle. The critical stages are at weaning and farrowing. It is important to be aware that although a good indicator of body fat cover, it does not correlate much better than 45 to 50 per cent to back fat thickness measured using ultra-sonography. Some studies show that this is as low as 32 per cent for the gilt after rearing its first litter. The so-called second litter syndrome of poor performance is frequently linked to inadequate gilt nutrition during the rearing stage, its first gestation and/or lactation.

All sows and gilts will lose body weight (fat and muscle) during lactation. The target maximum weight loss for a gilt rearing her first litter is 10 to 13 per cent between birth and weaning before this has a negative effect on her reproductive performance. For sows this should be well below 10 per cent (10 to 15kg is a good target). Ideally we would have two different gestation diets, one for younger sows and gilts, and one for older sows. Sows will continue to grow in body size until at least their fourth parity and especially during the first two gestations. Gilts and second gestation sows have a higher nutrient demand, especially for amino acids, compared with older sows. Younger sows need a diet higher in amino acids and a higher ratio of digestible lysine to energy to ensure an optimum development of muscles and back fat. Older sows need more energy for maintenance and to replenish weight loss during lactation.

However, it is usually only possible to feed all ages of sow a single gestation diet. This means a compromise has to be achieved between the young sows receiving more energy than they need and not enough amino acids, whilst older sows receive less energy and more amino acids than they require. This underlines the need to ensure an optimum body composition during replacement gilt rearing, ideally using a special diet. The opportunity to achieve ideal growth and condition during gestation is limited. The problem we have with older sows is that they have decreasing fat levels (lower body fat percentage) with an increased body mass, resulting in decreased energy reserves available for lactation. If these fat reserves fall too low during lactation, it will subsequently have a negative effect on the oestrous cycle and lead to infertility.

The challenge is to avoid this potential reduction in the sow's active lifespan, and ensure she can rear at least five or six productive litters before she is culled. There is no reason why the modern sow should not be able to rear seventy piglets during a six parity productive life.

GESTATION HOUSING AND FEEDING SYSTEMS

The requirement for sows and gilts to be kept in groups at all stages outside the farrowing period in the UK and some other EU countries, and after the first twenty-eight days of gestation in others, has led to the development of a range of housing and feeding systems. The type of housing and group sizes are very much dictated by the feeding method used and whether the sows are kept in so-called dynamic or static groups. Dynamic groups involve sows joining the large group at weaning, immediately after insemination, or after implantation is considered complete at just under twenty-one days of gestation; sows are removed in the week prior to their expected farrowing date. In static sow groups, all the sows are mated or inseminated to batch farrow within the same week.

Electronic sow feeder (ESF) systems have a recommended maximum of fifty sows per feeder, kept in either dynamic or static groups. Two or three computer-controlled feeders can be accessed by a large group of sows. Each sow carries a transponder (usually in the ear) and is recognized upon entry into the feeder, where she has her ration delivered into the trough. ESF systems can be based on straw or on slatted flooring in controlled environment housing. The example shown has natural ventilation.

ESF systems demand top class management and good heat-detection procedures, especially when the sows are kept in dynamic groups. These necessities put demands on managing this system that should not be underestimated, despite the fact that a computer screen is used to set individual feed rations. ESF feeders also require maintenance and ultimate replacement of the feeders.

An alternative is to use so-called 'dump' or 'spin' feeders suspended from the roof that either let the feed fall on to the solid floor or spread it further over a floor area, respectively: sows then have to root for their feed. Individual feeding is no longer possible and good monitoring of sow condition is essential. Unlike the ESF approach, the sow must feed relatively quickly at a fixed time determined by the pig keeper.

Small groups (four or five sows) and medium-sized groups (fifteen to twenty) can be fed using a variety of pen designs and feeding systems. Sows can be liquid fed in a communal trough for these group sizes. Feeding sows together in a trough using liquid feed works because the slower eater appears to be able to take in sufficient wet feed as compared to the often larger, more dominant pen mates. This is because it appears to 'fix' the individual sow, effectively forcing each one to concentrate on taking in its share within a short time frame (often less than ten minutes). Feeding sows the diet in a dry form does not achieve this desirable 'fixing' effect. Liquid feeding can also be automatically set at predetermined time intervals (often twice per day) when each trough is rapid filled.

An alternative system allows for dry meal to be dropped into an individual trough with shoulder barriers, and the meal is mixed with water in the trough. This 'fixes' the sows and ensures they consume their full and correct ration in about eight minutes. An example of this system is known as the 'Quickfeeder'. It looks very similar to the 'trickle feeder' system, but here dry feed is delivered slowly at about 120g per minute in a similar trough and pen arrangement, allowing each sow time to eat.

Another approach involves using a computer-controlled 'single-space' feeder that appears similar to those used for growing and finishing pigs. Between five and eight sows share one feeder, and sows must trigger a photoelectric cell to drop about 20 to 25g of feed at around 75sec intervals into the trough as determined by a computer

Straw-based ESF sow housing – the feeders are on the right-hand side. Note the sows have water drinkers mounted on the dividing wall.

input. This means the sow has to spend a number of hours eating its daily ration, mimicking natural feeding behaviour. The sow can add water to the feed using a nose-operated drinker. The computer controls the time that feed can be released, and how many grams fall after each timed electronic trigger. These feeders can be used for larger group sizes in larger pens, as shown in the photograph. This method works best with static groups of batch-farrowed sows.

Sows can enter and leave the free access cubicle or stall-based system whenever they like, as shown in the second photograph. There must be adequate space between the rows for the sows to enter and leave without hindrance. The system can be fully or partially slatted; the latter is preferable because it allows for the incorporation of a bedded area, and where this is available the sows will choose between the two options for resting, depending on the temperature. The photograph on page 177 shows a majority of the sows lying in the stalls during a hot summer day; but when the temperature falls at night or on cold days, they will lie on the bedded area and huddle together. This system is expensive to build from scratch, and difficult to fit into existing buildings. Adequate space per sow is essential for it to succeed. Sows are fed individually either manually or automatically, using dry or liquid feeds. Individual rationing is possible, depending on the feed used and the delivery system.

Outdoor sows are usually fed on the ground in both summer and winter. On larger units this is carried out using a mechanical feeder to distribute the large nuts or cobs into the paddock (*see* photograph).

A row of Atlantic 'Time-Mix' gestating sow feeders ('Domino' version). These are auger filled and controlled by a computer. Feed is released by a pneumatic (compressed air) system triggered by a light-sensitive cell.

Voluntary sow stalls are a very popular system for well insulated, environmentally controlled housing in some parts of Europe.

Static sow groups are easier to manage from a feed allocation and rationing perspective, both indoors and outdoors; furthermore they are easier to check for returns to service. Dynamic group systems are also used on outdoor units, but where this approach is chosen the management must be appropriate and of a sufficiently high standard to ensure good results.

The sow housing and feeding methods described above are good examples of many of those currently in use, and illustrate how adaptable breeding pigs can be. The feeding system and appropriate diet specifications will determine the layout and operation of the gestating sow housing layout and facilities, and expert advice and practical experience gained prior to operating any of these systems is essential for their success.

Average feed consumption per sow per year in UK indoor herds (2013) is recorded at 1.2 tonnes, whilst outdoor herds average 1.36 tonnes per sow per year. The outdoor sow requires 160kg more than an indoor sow, and is effectively at least 13 per cent more expensive to feed on average. This feed allocation includes the feed used by breeding boars. Where 100 per cent AI is used there is a saving for boar feed, and adjusting for this gives about 8 per cent more feed

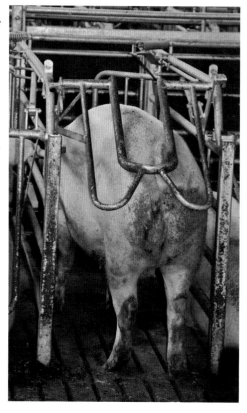

View of free access sow feeder/ resting stalls and the large exercise area and bedded area. This is designed to allow sows to rest and sleep together if they want to. The second photo shows how the sow can enter and leave her stall at will. Some variants have sow-operated saloon door rear gates. Both systems ensure that a sow cannot be attacked from behind whilst feeding or resting inside her individual stall.

consumed by the outdoor sow if all indoor herds used AI and outdoor herds none. The cost of the extra boars outdoors is a factor, but the effect of cold wet conditions, more energy outdoors for exercise, and feed wastage during feeding, must account for at least three-quarters of the higher consumption.

Feeding sows an ad-lib diet during lactation is also an approach used outdoors and sometimes indoors, but not normally during gestation. Ad-lib feeding of sows during gestation using a very low nutrient density feed (that is, low energy and protein with balanced micro-nutrients) has been used successfully in the Netherlands, where the feed ingredients required to achieve this diet profile could be bought in economically. It has not been found to be a successful approach in most other countries due to the high cost of producing the diet and a perceived difficulty in maintaining optimum sow body condition.

Outdoor sows need a large-sized feed roll or cob. This makes it easier for the sow to locate them and eat them in wet, muddy conditions and reduces waste, especially as they are not so easy for birds to eat. A feed controller is located in the tractor cab to allow the operator to set the correct feed allocation to each paddock. ATV versions are also available for the smaller unit. Feeding by hand is a labour-intensive process, and using feed in bags is also expensive.

ACHIEVING OPTIMUM RETURNS

Ultimately, the gestating sow management system chosen must provide for the specific needs of the gilts, sows and boars. Feeding the breeding herd correctly and appropriately demands top class nutrition, management and an effective feeding system. All of the examples shown in the photographs were from herds with very high levels of animal welfare and breeding performance. Several of these produce in excess of thirty pigs per sow per year.

The pig is an adaptable animal, but it must be managed effectively to achieve an optimum return. Regardless of the system used we should aim at an average of at least five parities achieved by each sow (five litters reared) in her lifetime. We can calculate the percentage of the sow herd that is replaced each year by dividing average parity by the average number of litters weaned per sow per year (farrowing index) to give the herd life of each sow in years: for example, 5 divided by 2.38 = 2.1 years; the percentage replacement rate will be 100 divided by 2.1 = 47.6 per cent.

On this basis, for each 100 sows we will replace about forty-eight sows with gilts each year. This means that at least four gilts must be confirmed in pig each month to keep close to a target of twenty litters per month (240 per annum, or 2.4 per sow) for each 100 sows kept in the herd. This will require five or six gilts to be inseminated or mated each month per 100 sows.

Aim for just under half the herd to be in parities three to five, because these are the most productive breeding animals.

It is recommended to have a maiden gilt pool equal to 12 per cent of the breeding herd size (twelve gilts per 100 sows). This gilt pool should be increased slightly where seasonal infertility demands more gilt inseminations to maintain farrowing numbers, and piglets weaned at the required level.

See page 106 for details about feeding the boar.

FURTHER INFORMATION

Further reading and web/smartphone links:
www.bpex.org.uk/2TS/breeding
Practical Pig App – play.google.com and search BPEX Practical Pig.
Videos can also be downloaded at: practicalpig.bpex.org.uk
Essential further reading: *Nutrition of Sows and Boars* by W.H. Close and D.J.A. Cole, 2003.
Also advice for owners keeping pigs as pets or 'micro' pigs can be obtained from: www.rspca.org.uk and www.defra.gov.uk/ahvla-en/files/pub-pigs-micro-pet.pdf
How big do 'micro' pigs get: lancashiremicropigs.co.uk/how-big-do-micro-pigs-get-micro-pig-height-size-explained/
Why feeding kitchen waste is illegal: www.npa-uk.org.uk/disease.html?gclid=CLm60tPIwbkCFXQftAodDGQAvw

Large rolls used to feed outdoor breeding pigs.

9

Health and Welfare

The pig keeper must learn to observe normal and abnormal behaviour in pigs. Symptoms of disease include changes in the animal's behaviour, its dung, vomit, skin/coat, eyes, ears and nose, respiration rate and rectal temperature. Other symptoms include tail and ear biting and navel and ear sucking. Gilts, and occasionally sows, will attack and savage their piglets at birth. True cannibalism is rarer, but can cause heavy losses when a sow that farrows in a group (outdoor pigs) consumes her own or other sows' offspring. Such sows should be culled immediately. In general, a sick pig will be reluctant to eat, will usually lie down, and may tremble or have skin discoloration. Constipation or scouring, coughing, breathing heavily (blowing) and staggering are also symptoms of illness.

DISEASES AND DISORDERS

Disease is usually present, in one form or another, in every pig herd large and small, whether it includes breeding and finishing rare breeds, pedigree stock, or commercial hybrids. Infectious diseases are caused by viruses, bacteria, mycoplasmas and parasites. Non-infectious causes of disease will range from dietary deficiencies or excesses (toxic effects) and mycotoxins in feed and bedding, fumonsins and deoxynivalenol vomitoxin in feed, genetic disease and physiological/metabolic imbalances and disorders. We describe the effects of a disease based on the level of morbidity and the mortality rate: morbidity is the percentage of the population affected, and mortality the percentage of the population killed by the disease.

The following directory provides an outline of diseases and disorders found in pigs:

Gastrointestinal Disorders

E. coli is the typical cause of diarrhoea (scours) in young pigs, bowel oedema in weaned pigs, and colitis in young pigs. Scours are often triggered by a lack of hygiene or some other aspect of management connected with the environment or feeding. The pathogenic organisms then capitalize on the situation, attacking the villi lining the small intestines. They multiply very quickly, doubling in number every twenty minutes; thus one coli can become 17 million in eight hours. Some other causes of diarrhoea are TGE, epidemic diarrhoea type II, coccidiosis, rotaviral enteritis (three strains), *Clostridium welchii* type C (difficile and perfringens type A), swine dysentery, salmonellosis or cryptosporidia.

Ileitis is one of the most common enteric diseases found in grower and finishing pigs. It is caused by *Lawsonia intracellularis*, which can result in a 10 per cent reduction in weight gain, can affect up to 40 per cent of pigs with diarrhoea, with normal-looking pigs having a poorer feed efficiency and greater variation in weight. This variation can lead to tremendous losses at slaughter due to underweight pigs, especially if an all-in, all out slaughter policy is adopted.

Since early May 2013 USA pig herds have been suffering from a new strain of **porcine epidemic diarrhoea virus (PEDV)**. This is a type of coronavirus and it caused problems in the UK in the 1970s and 1980s. PEDV kills 80 to 100 per cent of the piglets it infects. There is no vaccine and the only defence is a natural build-up of immunity. It is thought to have originated in China in 2010 and may have evolved from a virus found in bats.

NNPD, or **new neonatal porcine diarrhoea**, was documented in Denmark as early as 2008, though in 2013 it was still unclear what causes it. A virus is suspected, but it is considered a syndrome requiring a good living environment, optimized hygiene and an adjustment to the diet nutrient density, feeding rate and feed protein content. Extra colostrum and antibiotics are considered to be appropriate treatments.

Vomiting in suckling pigs may be caused by vomiting and wasting disease (Coronavirus), TGE (Coronavirus), rotaviral enteritis or (in older pigs) mycotoxins/vomitoxins, Glässers disease (*Haemophilus parasuis*), strongyle worms, gastric ulcers or toxic substances. **Rectal prolapse** may be caused by diarrhoea, constipation, water shortage, coughing, zearalenone (mycotoxin), floor design (excessively sloped), huddling or piling of cold pigs (pressure is exerted on the rectum of the pig at the bottom of the pile) or feed antibiotics. It may also occur post farrowing, due to various causes. It can happen from one to two days old and at any age.

Most **pig worm problems** are caused by *Ascaris suum* (round-worm), *Hyostrongylus rubidus* (stomach worm), *Oesophagostomum dentatum/ quadrispinulatum* (intestinal worms), *Metastrongylus* (lung-worm in outdoor pigs) or *Trichuris suis* (whipworm of the caecum and large intestine). These are all easily controlled with anthelmintics and should not pose a problem, but do keep an eye out for worms. The liver is also affected by migrating parasites (for example Ascarid larvae causing milk spots), bacterial septicaemia, viruses and nu-tritional disorders (mycotoxins and fatty liver). Also implicated is PMWS/PCV2 (circovirus).

Respiratory Diseases

Respiratory diseases have a considerable economic impact. Like the digestive system, the respiratory tract is easily damaged and infected in poor environments or under poor management. Pleurisy is found in a high proportion of slaughter pigs and testifies to an underlying disease problem in the pig's lungs.

Respiratory distress in unweaned pigs is likely to be caused by iron deficiency (anaemia), *Bordetella bronchiseptica* pneumonia, *Hae-mophilus pleuropneumoniae* and *mycoplasma pneumonia* (both common in slaughter pigs), toxoplasmosis, barking piglet syndrome (at birth) or streptococcus. Added causes in weaned and older pigs are por-cine stress syndrome, swine influenza, and damage by worms of the *Ascaris suum* and *Metastrongylus* species as they migrate via the lungs.

Sneezing in unweaned, weaned and older pigs is likely to be due to **rhinitis**, which can develop into atrophic rhinitis (AR). *Bordetella bronchiseptica* and *pasteurella multocida* are the cause, probably together with body rhinitis (cytomegalovirus). Contaminants in the environment such as dust or ammonia may aggravate AR or cause a mild inflammation of the respiratory epithelium. Keeping fewer animals in an air space, especially baby pigs, and maintaining good ventilation will help.

PRRS or **blue ear** also remains a problem. Since at least 1999 in the UK, PMWS/PCV2 (circovirus) has proved to be an economically devastating disease syndrome that attacks the immune system in the lung itself.

Disorders Affecting the External Body

Infections, conditions and infestations affecting the external body include lice, mange (sarcoptic and sometimes demodectic), ringworm, rashes and 'diamonds' (acute erysipelas); also callous of the knee, fetlock, elbow or hock; mastitis, and piglet teat and knee erosion; abscesses; ringworm; sunburn and greasy pig disease (*Staphylococcus hyicus*); foot and mouth disease, PDNS/PCV2, swinepox (a vesicular disease); and parakeratosis, due to excess calcium suppressing zinc availability in the diet.

Disorders Affecting the Nervous System

Infections and conditions affecting the nervous system include behavioural abnormalities, lack of co-ordination, paralysis, tremors, paddling, dog sitting, convulsions, streptococcal meningitis (*Streptococcus suis*) and *E. coli* toxins (oedema disease); also deafness, splay leg, blindness and coma-death (for example salt poisoning due to lack of water or salt toxicosis).

Disorders Affecting the Eyes

Infections and conditions affecting the eyes include **conjunctivitis**, and weeping, as a result of, for example, dusty eyes (rhinitis). **Oedema disease** (enterotoxaemia by *E. coli*) produces swollen eyelids.

Systemic Disease

Systemic disease involves sudden death (numerous diseases), wasting and ill thrift, anaemia, navel bleeding in baby piglets, and mycotoxins.

Disorders of the Cardiovascular System

Disorders of the cardiovascular system include **mulberry heart disease (MHD)**, due to vitamin E/selenium deficiency and pro-inflammatory fatty acids. Chronic erysipelas causes **endocarditis**, with cauliflower lesions on the heart valves.

Musculoskeletal Disorders

These disorders include lameness (for example chronic erysipelas or arthritis), white muscle disease, porcine stress syndrome, rickets, osteochondrosis, osteoporosis.

Reproductive and Urogenital Disorders

Conditions affecting the reproductive and urogenital systems include SMEDI (enteroviruses) – abortion, small litters, stillbirth and mummified piglets and infertility – parvovirus, PRRS (blue ear), bacteria and moulds, agalactia, metritis (*E. coli*, streptococcus, klebsiella), cystitis and nephritis due to *Actinobaculum suis* (previously known as Corynibacterium,) also sometimes *E. coli*, PDNS/PCV2, bacterial septicaemia (salmonella, erysipelas), parasites, *urate nephrosis*.

Genetic and Congenital Disorders

These disorders include scrotal and umbilical hernias or ruptures, *atresia ani* (no anus), splay leg, *pityriasis rosea* (skin condition), kinky tail, *dermatosis vegetans* and trembling.

Notifiable Diseases

Notifiable diseases include African swine fever, anthrax, Aujeszky's disease, foot and mouth disease, rabies, classical swine fever, swine vesicular disease, Teschen disease (porcine enterovirus encephalomyelitis). African swine fever had reached the eastern EU in 2013.

Cystitis/Nephritis in Sows (Pyelo-Nephritis)

Cystitis is one of the biggest killers of sows in the UK and in many other countries. Experts believe that it is an environmental disease caused by organisms in and around the sow, with housing systems as the root cause. If the infection gets to the kidneys then it will develop into the killer form, nephritis. The organism believed to be associated with this disease is *Corynebacterium suis*, as it is usually found in the dead sows. *See* next section for the control of cystitis.

HEALTH CONTROL

Vaccines and Vaccination Programmes

As has been indicated, many diseases are influenced by the quality of the environment and management. For certain diseases, a vaccination programme arranged by your vet will help maintain herd health.

Examples of Vaccines for Viral Diseases

Vaccines are available for the control of Aujeszky's disease, foot and mouth disease, porcine circovirus Type II (PCV2), porcine parvovirus, PRRS (porcine reproductive and respiratory syndrome), swine fever, swine influenza H1N1, H1N2, or H3N2 – Gripovac 3 vaccine, TGE.

Examples of Vaccines for Bacterial (and Mycoplasma) Diseases

Vaccines are also available for the control of *Actinobacillus pleuropneumoniae*, anthrax (Northern Ireland only), atrophic rhinitis, Aujeszky's disease (eradicated in mainland Britain), clostridial enteritis (*C. welchii* type C), *Clostridium oedematiens* (*novyi*) type B, colibacillosis (*E. coli* scours), erysipelas, *Haemophilus parasuis* (Glasser's disease), mycoplasma, pasteurella, parvovirus, salmonella, *Streptococcus suis*, *Spahylococcus hyicus* (greasy pig disease). Some of these are only available as autogenous vaccines produced for a specific situation.

The use of some vaccines against notifiable diseases will make it impossible for that country to subsequently demonstrate that a disease such as foot and mouth (FMD) is not present. Recent (2013) research from the Netherlands shows that a single FMD vaccination in pigs does not stop the virus spreading. This was considered to be due to the high pressure of infection in pigs. The use of vaccines for notifiable diseases will almost certainly result in that country suffering export restrictions that would prohibit breeding stock sales and even meat exports for a number of years at least.

Vaccines can be used directly to stimulate and provide active immunity in an individual or group, and to provide indirect passive immunity for the offspring via the colostrum.

Atrophic rhinitis vaccine: This is a disease of the pig's turbinate bones, which filter the air and act as heat exchangers inside its snout. The infected pig has a high chance of getting one of the chronic pneumonias, and growing and converting its food very poorly. Environmental conditions in the farrowing and weaning accommodation have a tremendous influence. Vaccination may be the only way to control this disease, and the vaccines available offer protection against some of the Bordetella strains (for example Porcilis AR-T DF) and also include pasteurella. The best results appear to be gained when the sows and gilts are vaccinated in order to pass on the immunity to their piglets. Reducing dust levels and keeping stocking rates down will also help with this chronic disorder.

E. coli **(otherwise known as Colibacillosis) vaccines:** These vaccines are designed to control certain strains of the *Escherichia coli* which are very common in the gut of the young pig, and are passed out in vast numbers by the sow at farrowing. The most severe disease incidence manifests itself as a frequently fatal diarrhoea, occurring in young piglets often within days of birth, and up to or after weaning. Oedema disease is an enterotoxaemia caused by certain strains of *E. coli*: an exotoxin gets into the blood and damages the blood vessel walls, resulting in oedema.

Vaccines for clostridial organisms: These organisms are well known to shepherds, and *Clostridium perfrigens* can also be a serious cause of piglet scours. The organism lives in the soil. Serious thought should be given to vaccinating young pigs fattened outdoors. *Cl. novyi* infection can cause sudden death in sows. The liver will appear bubbly (Aero chocolate) on post-mortem examination. *Cl. tetani* causes tetanus, and *Cl. botulinum* causes botulism. Take veterinary advice on a suitable vaccine to use (for example Covexin). *Cl. novyi* has no licensed vaccine for pigs (2013), but a version may be available 'off licence' under strict veterinary prescription.

Erysipelas vaccine: Erysipelas is a classic example where vaccines have been available for many years for most serotypes, but even in 2013 it is not used in all breeding herds. Vaccination only provides protection for a short time. It is a common disease and unfortunately it continues to go unrecognized on many farms.

Porcine parvovirus vaccines: These vaccines tend to be used only in gilts to effectively control the herd infertility syndrome, often referred to as a SMEDI problem. PRRS (blue ear) continues to be economically damaging – vaccines are available for this fast mutating virus (for example Porcilis PRRS). PCV2 vaccines (for example Suvaxyn PCV) are usually used on sows, but some farms find a benefit also from vaccinating piglets at weaning. PCV2 is implicated as a causal agent for PMWS and PDNS.

Salmonella cholera-suis is covered by the Zoonoses Order in the UK, and there are no vaccines available for use in the UK in 2013, but they do exist. Salmonella is subject to a ZAP monitoring programme in the UK.

Implementing a Vaccination Programme

Failure of any vaccine may be due to poor injection technique or poor colostrum intake by the piglet. In the first instance, approach the problem based on hygiene, the environment and management: any vaccination programme will flounder if appropriate attention is not paid to improvements in nutrition, housing and general hygiene.

Remember to read the directions on the label and obtain instruction if new techniques are required. If properly carried out, vaccination is a very useful tool in disease prevention and control. However, vaccines can have considerable limitations, and new variants of the pathogen can develop that are not immediately covered by the existing vaccine. Vaccines developed using advanced molecular biotechnology techniques may offer new possibilities in the future. Needle-free vaccine injection devices are also available and may well become popular.

It is essential that all vaccination programmes and procedures are carried out correctly under veterinary supervision.

Iron Supplementation

The piglet has one of the fastest growth rates of any species, and during the first three weeks of life a typical piglet will have gained up to five times its birth weight. The demand for iron in piglets is far greater than in other animals. The total amount needed to maintain reasonable growth and prevent anaemia during the first three weeks of life has been calculated at between 250 and 350mg.

If a piglet is reared away from soil or any other source of iron, it will begin to develop a deficiency within the first week of life. In fact, the piglet is born with just 50mg of iron in its body, and suckling mother's milk for three weeks will only add around 25mg. To this you must add what it picks up from the environment, which will include the sow's dung if soil is not available. Trials show that piglets will eat up to 20g of their mother's dung each day, and in cases where the mother has a high iron intake, piglets have been known to get adequate iron from this source.

Sufficient iron intake from the environment is virtually impossible for a piglet indoors. It is also frequently not as successful outdoors as many believe, because it is effectively a hit-and-miss approach. Trials have shown that on average, outdoor pigs are 0.26kg heavier at weaning when given an iron injection. This improvement was greater in the winter months when the piglets are less likely to spend enough time outside rooting in the soil. We can probably rely on the environment providing no more than 50mg per piglet indoors and often well short of the 250 to 300mg they need outdoors. This leaves a deficit of between 100 and 200mg, and explains why indoor pig keepers normally supplement 200mg of iron within four days of birth.

Oral iron on day one of life using a micro-emulsion that is absorbed just like the sow's colostrum has been available and used highly successfully for some time in the UK (FeVit). Piglets in Denmark often receive iron as a constant nutritional supplement, in water or as a dry powder whilst suckling. The smaller 1ml dose is safer than the old 2ml iron dextran injections, which can cause a fatal reaction in small piglets in particular, and lead to chronic joint infections and inflammation. Iron compounds should be injected into the ham for best results. The neck is preferred by some people, although the iron is less well absorbed because of the mixture of fat and muscle in that part of the animal.

Iron supplementation, given either orally or injected, will almost invariably produce heavier pigs at weaning. These pigs will also reach heavier slaughter weights more rapidly and economically. If piglets appear 'chalky' white at around fourteen days of age, give them another 200mg injection, or an oral supplementation. In 2013, investing 10p/piglet for iron supplementation for an outdoor piglet can produce a return of more than £1 per pig at slaughter. Indoors, it has to be an absolutely standard procedure.

Controlling Cystitis/Nephritis in Sows (Pyelo-Nephritis)

Cystitis deserves attention because it one of the biggest killers of sows in the UK and in many other countries. Experts believe that it is an environmental disease caused by organisms in and around the sow, with housing systems as the root cause. If the infection gets to the kidneys then it will develop into the killer form, nephritis. Reduced water intake is also implicated, and it is essential to ensure that sows get a flow rate of at least a litre per minute, if using nipple or bite drinkers. Some people advocate a slight increase in diet salt, which in theory should increase thirst and subsequent drinking. However, take care with this advice because salt poisoning also kills.

The organism believed to be associated with this disease is *Corynebacterium suis*, as it is usually found in the dead sows. This organism has been found in the sheath (prepuce) of a high proportion of boars – indeed, it was found in thirty-two out of thirty-three wild boars tested in Germany. It is uncertain whether the boar spreads the organism during mating, but there is some evidence to link certain boars with sow infections and there is a suggestion that long-legged boars damage the entrance to the sow's urethra.

Like many diseases it is a multi-factorial problem and is likely to be linked to increasing intensification, early weaning, poor service area hygiene, cross mating of boars, high sow density and continual throughput in the service area. Poor AI techniques and lack of AI hygiene are also implicated. The use of sulpha-type drugs in sow feed may also predispose to this disease, because they are passed out as small crystals in the urine. The disease can kill, but the usual symptoms are a sow off her feed with a vaginal discharge, which will respond rapidly to an antibiotic injection. Damage to the kidneys may be severe, so do discuss with your veterinary surgeon whether the animal should be culled or retained for further breeding.

Controlling Mange and Lice

There should be no lice on any modern self-respecting pig farm, but in the event of infestation there are a number of products available that will give an excellent kill. Mange mites burrow deep into the skin and cause considerable irritation and secondary infection, resulting in reduced animal performance and welfare. There are pour-on products, injectable products (also wormer) and spray-on materials. If attacked from all angles it should be possible to virtually eradicate this skin pest on your farm. Boars are often to blame for passing on mange, so treat them regularly. Talk to a specialist vet about mange control. Treatments must be regular and thorough. If restocking, buy pigs from mange- and lice-free sources. Mange treatment also controls lice.

Controlling Worms

Anthelmintics are available in the UK based on two active chemicals – avermectins and benzimidazoles. The avermectins include Ivomectin (in feed and injectable) and Doramectin (injectable only). The benzimidazoles include Flubendazole (in feed, top dressing and in water) and Fenbendazole (in feed and direct oral application).

There is no excuse for a worm problem building up on any pig farm, and it is the duty of every pig keeper to plan and execute appropriate worming and worm monitoring programmes together with their veterinary surgeon.

Hygiene Procedures

Sunlight, fresh air and time are probably the best disinfectants and should be used whenever possible. If the opportunity arises to restock a pig unit, then a rest period of at least six weeks is recommended. If the previous herd had swine dysentery you should allow eight weeks, or the time scale dictated by the authorities. The farrowing and weaner accommodation areas tend to be most prone to disease, and they deserve a planned hygiene programme in every herd.

You should always try to operate an all-in, all-out policy, allowing several days in which to clean out a house or compartment within a house. Use water to wet the area and de-greasing detergents to enable the pressure washer to operate more gently when removing dirt. If used correctly, pressure washers can be a great help, but they can also do untold damage to a concrete surface, which would later injure the pig. Use approved disinfectants to back up a cleaning job and not in an attempt to skimp on elbow grease.

Disinfectants do not work in dirt (and that includes dirty boots). German research indicates that most disinfectants do not work at temperatures around 10°C or below. You should aim to keep house temperatures at 20°C for effective disinfectant action.

Fumigation is also useful. Boot and floor disinfection using a powder disinfectant works at sub-zero temperatures and is effective against PRRSv – for example Stalosan F.

Always start cleaning at the top, with the ceiling, and work down to floor level. Take every opportunity to clean the drinking-water tank, and use a special-purpose disinfectant to clean the circulation pipes and drinkers from within. Take as much equipment as possible outside and allow the sun, rain and fresh air to get at them. Cube drinkers should be scrubbed and then soaked in a bath of disinfectant for a few days.

Do not forget the feed bins: fumigate them frequently, and where possible, pressure wash from the inside. Augers can be cleaned by allowing clean sand to circulate.

Hygiene procedure really is a never-ending task, but avoid it at your peril!

Safety must be paramount at all times, especially electrical safety when dealing with water and electrical heaters. Always use residual current circuit breakers when using pressure washers.

Health Schemes and Veterinary Consultants

Various pig health schemes are operated in order to coordinate and monitor the health of the national and local pig populations. NADIS was formed in 1995 to promote animal health and welfare

Recommended Needle Sizes for Use in Pigs

AGE	INTRAMUSCULAR		SUBCUTANEOUS	
	Gauge	Length (mm)	Gauge	Length (mm)
Birth to 7kg	21	15	21	15
7–25kg	19	25	21	15
25–60	19	25	19	12
60–100kg	16	38	19	19
Adult pigs	16	38	16	19

Castration

The majority of male pigs in the UK are no longer castrated, despite a move to a larger European slaughter weight. In any event, the practice is due to be restricted across the whole of the EU. A (non-disease) vaccine has been available for some time and used on entire males in Australia. The vaccine acts on the gonadotrophin-releasing hormone and temporarily destroys GnRH, which then limits the production of testosterone. This shrinks the testicles, reduces male behaviour and cuts down on boar taint. It may become a routine in EU countries in due course.

It is essential, although not yet law, for all persons over eighteen years of age to attend a training course at an agricultural college or other recognized course prior to castrating any pigs. Persons below eighteen are not allowed to castrate any animal, although seventeen-year-olds may be instructed by a veterinary surgeon or qualified college or training scheme instructor. Castrating cannot be learnt from a book, so be sure to receive adequate instruction and to have your competence formally assessed and recognized for this, and other tasks, under the Pig Industry Professional Register (PIPR) run by City and Guilds (formerly NPTC), and as part of your continued professional development.

Ringing

There are two types of ring designed to prevent excessive rooting in outdoor breeding sows. These are septum rings (bull rings; *see* page 200), and rings placed around the 'rooting disc' of the nose. The septum ring probably causes less pain. Many outdoor herds can operate without nose rings and can usually avoid serious soil damage. Boars are not normally ringed. Again, it is essential for persons to be trained before ringing pigs.

Teeth Clipping

Teeth clipping is frequently a necessary task in modern pig production when sows are feeding more than eight piglets. Some litters do not damage each other or the sow, but it would be both cruel and bad husbandry not to take steps against biting and fighting where it is a problem. Wounds from bites can cause both local and more serious infections, which could end up with the death of a piglet.

Teeth clipping (or tip grinding) is best carried out within the first twenty-four hours of life using a clean pair of clippers or forceps, which should be dipped in a suitable antiseptic medium (for example Chlorhexidine and cetrimide in alcohol). There are eight needle-sharp teeth, consisting of four front incisors and four canines. Cutting them has no effect on the further development of the pig's twenty-eight temporary teeth. These are followed, at about fourteen

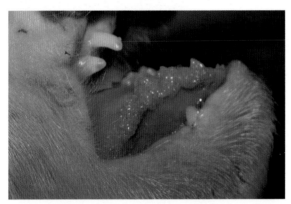

Piglets are born with eight needle-sharp teeth.

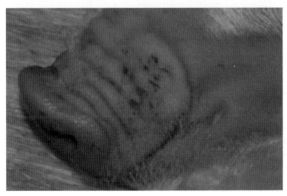

Damage done to a piglet's nose through fighting within a few hours of birth and before the needle-sharp teeth were removed.

197

After only a day or so there are signs of infection and further injury in this piglet from a litter not teeth clipped shortly after birth.

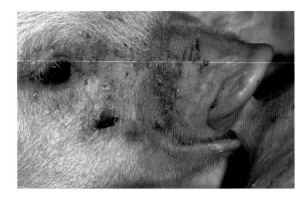

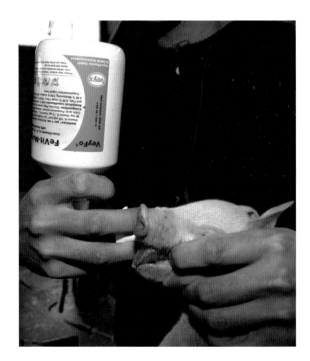

A piglet receiving its 2ml dose of oral iron shortly after it has taken in its first feed of colostrum. This is a viable alternative to injecting the iron supplement.

weeks of age, by its next set of teeth. Each adult jaw will contain six molars, eight pre-molars, two canines (tusks in the male), and six incisors.

It is important to hold the piglet correctly and to cut the tooth, which is quite soft at this stage, down to just above, but without damaging, the gum. Although the law does not demand it, attendance on a training course would be well advised prior to teeth clipping on your own. There is an on-going debate about whether clipping or grinding is the more acceptable from a welfare point of view. It is also possible to stop teeth clipping altogether with some pig breed/strains, but the ultimate decision either way must be whether or not the welfare of the piglet and sow is compromised.

Tail Docking Young Pigs

Tail docking has been described as a 'necessary mutilation', where tail biting cannot be controlled by any other means. UK regulations state that tail docking must not be a routine procedure, but it is permitted under veterinary guidance where the problem of tail biting in growing pigs cannot be controlled by other methods. Unfortunately pigs have very little feeling in the top one-third of their tails, and do not react quickly enough to prevent them being bitten to the point of bleeding. The taste of blood then sets the others off, and pigs can be severely injured.

Stockholm tar painted on the tail was the traditional remedy in the nineteenth century, and can still be used to put the others off, but once a tail is injured infections can enter and cause abscesses of the spine. These can make an animal lame, cause great pain, and almost invariably lead to the carcase being condemned for human consumption. Improving and enriching the pen environment may help reduce the incidence, but even small numbers of pigs in a free-range situation have been known to tail bite.

There are known to be many causes of tail biting, but a blueprint for preventing it will probably always elude us. If it is seen to commence in a pen, then try throwing in a paper bag or straw, or even an old football to distract attention. If you can identify the perpetrator, remove it from the pen immediately. The injured animal(s) should be moved to a hospital pen, and may require veterinary treatment.

Make sure that the environment is adequate, with few draughts and variations in temperature. Feed and water supply is critical, along with a correct balance of nutrients. The pigs require adequate floor space (the minimum is defined in law), described as stocking density. Illness and disease may also be part of the complex pathological and physiological cause of the malcontent and aggression that leads to the vice of tail biting. On the basis of a survey of some fourteen pig veterinary specialists covering 400,000 pigs, NADIS (2013) reported that the incidence of tail biting was 0.4 per cent on straw-based systems and over 2 per cent on slatted floor-ing. Outdoor-born pigs were less likely to tail bite than those born indoors. The overall average for these was just over 1 per cent on slats.

Tail docking must be carried out by the time the pig is seven days old, and ideally within the first few days. If the pig is over that age, removal of part of its tail to prevent injury from tail biting or on health grounds by anyone other than a vet, is ille-gal – although you may have to do so as a first-aid measure in an emergency. It was normal practice to remove approximately 20mm from the baby pig's tail, ensuring that at least 12mm re-mained; it is now recommended in the UK to leave 20mm and remove only about 10mm.

There is also evidence that uneven tail lengths tend to increase the risk of tail biting, with the longer tails being more likely to be affected. Ask your veterinary surgeon for advice on this, and with regard to applying antiseptic to the tail stump. Opinion is divided, as some experts believe that antiseptics can actually act as an irri-tant. The tail can be cut with special sharp clippers, or using a hot cauterizing tool. Both methods are effective, and there is very little difference in the apparent post treatment behaviour of the piglets, but human opinions vary.

Identification Procedures

Identification of individual animals is required in law, in pedi-gree herds and those involved in breed improvement schemes. The

Two types of plastic ear tag, a visible tattoo number and a nose ring used on outdoor JSR breeding gilts.

pedigree breed societies (BPA) have differing rules on identification and number sequences. Ear tattoos, ear tags and ear notching are permitted by the various breed societies. *See also* Chapter 2 'The Market'. www.gov.uk/pigs-identification-registration-and-movement

Ear tags: Tags must be fitted away from veins and in a position where they will not catch easily in fencing or undergrowth. They are usually fitted with purpose-made pliers. Ear tag-mounted transponders for computer-controlled feed stations are also used; these incorporate reusable transponder units.

Electronic identification: Collars carrying transponders or responders for electronic feeding systems were the original method of electronic identification. Electronic implants are also available. These are injected into a fold of skin at the base of the ear and provide an electronic number for each pig, rather like an electronic bar code on shop items.

Ear notching: Like teeth clipping, ear notching can be carried out single-handed using a set of special pliers, often including a hole punch. Always remind yourself of the notch positions required for each particular pig – once a notch is cut it cannot be repositioned. This method of identification has been used for thousands of years on ears all over the world. It is a very rapid method of identifying a pig at a distance without having to restrain it, and useful in coloured breeds where ear tattoos are difficult to read.

Ear tattoos: These tattoos are an excellent method of permanent identification in piglets of white breeds from three days onwards using an 8mm (also 10mm for older piglets) tattoo die using green ink.

Slap marking: This method is used with 16mm dies and black ink for slaughter pigs and culled breeding stock; the mark is generally made on the shoulder.

For pedigree registration download:
www.britishpigs.org.uk/recordingandID.pdf and also
www.thepigsite.com/pighealth/article/561/identification-tattooing-slap-marking-tagging-etc.

Ear notching – used to enter various number codes in pigs' ears.

Ear notching – the end result used in combination with a plastic ear tag. This shows the national herd registration number and the sow's own identification number.

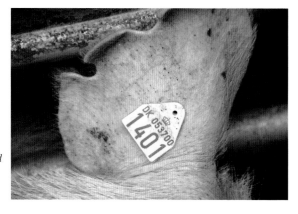

WELFARE

Animal welfare is an emotive topic and it can mean all manner of things to different people. All self-respecting keepers of live-stock would claim to have their animals' welfare at heart, and in almost every circumstance the performance of animals will improve when welfare conditions are good. Before looking at the rules and regulations governing welfare, it is worth defining any negative aspects that occur when animals are ill-treated. Roger Ewbank of the UFAW has defined the ill-treatment of animals as follows:

- Abuse (deliberate): injury, pain, fear – economic loss
- Ill-treatment: neglect (idleness, ignorance, overwork) – for example malnutrition, overcrowding
- Disease: discomfort – economic loss
- Deprivation: restriction

The problems of abuse and neglect can occur with anyone whether they keep one or one hundred pigs. The problem area is that of deprivation. This is frequently defined as depriving an animal of a behavioural or physical need, which results in the clinical signs of pain, discomfort, distress, disease and so on. If the offence is clear, then it was already prosecutable under the Protection of Animals Act 1911, or the Agriculture (Misc. Prov.) Act 1968.

In practice, deprivation is the most difficult form of ill-treatment to deal with, and animals would undoubtedly disagree with what a committee of human experts considers to be deprivation. Since 1 January 2013 it has been illegal to keep sows in permanent con-finement in 'sow stalls' after the first twenty-eight days of gestation in any EU country. This 'partial ban' is the minimum, but countries such as the UK and Sweden have long had a total ban on confine-ment at any stage apart from farrowing. The UK has very strict enforcement, but this may not always be the case in other EU coun-tries operating only a partial ban.

The UK government's own Farm Animal Welfare Council was re-sponsible for producing the welfare codes. The FAWC was disbanded on 31 March, 2011, and has been replaced by several 'standing com-mittees' and the Pig Health and Welfare Council. The codes of recom-mendation for the welfare of livestock cover all farmed species and still apply, even though they do not lay down statutory requirements. However, the farmer is legally obliged to ensure that all staff attending to their pigs are familiar with, and have access to, the welfare code for pigs. The codes may also be used to back up legislative requirements, such as when a person is accused of a welfare offence. Failure to comply with the code may be relied upon by the prosecution to establish guilt.

In addition, the person attending the livestock, on behalf of the owner, must have received appropriate guidance and instruction with regard to any such code. The farmer should also be familiar with the laws relating to animal welfare, whilst the persons looking after the animals must take immediate action when welfare is compromised. Welfare issues are outlined in the instruction 'Cross Compliance and Duty of Care to Pigs' in The Animal Welfare Act 2006: this is based on the 'five freedoms' from the 'Welfare Codes for Pigs', and specifically states that an animal's welfare needs include the following:

- A suitable environment (how it is housed)
- A suitable diet (what it eats and drinks – provision of water)
- The ability to exhibit normal behaviour patterns
- Any need it has to be housed with, or apart from, other animals
- Protection from pain, suffering, injury and disease

In England (Scotland, Northern Ireland and Wales will have equivalent laws where appropriate), The Welfare of Farmed Animals (England) Regulations 2007 were made under the Animal Welfare Act 2006 and provide additional protection for farmed animals. Schedule 8 of these regulations covers the additional welfare requirements for the keeping of pigs, and implements EU Council directive 91/630/EEC (as amended). It is important for all pig keepers to familiarize themselves with the up-to-date rules, regulations and laws relating to animal welfare. For example, further details regarding 'environmental enrichment' for pigs will be made available by the EU during the spring of 2014.

The UK Red Tractor Assurance Scheme already includes a 'Real Welfare' assessment, and this includes the confirmation that environmental enrichment objects are in use. They define this with the 'six Ss', confirming that they must be safe, sanitary, suspended, soft, simple and (correctly) sited. See: www.bpex.org.uk/downloads/301028/298574/Environment%20Enrichment%20for%20Pigs.pdf

Casualty Slaughter

Casualty slaughter regulations apply to all animals and are particularly important for pig keepers when arranging the humane slaughter of casualty animals. The procedures and decision-making process on whether a pig is fit enough for sale for slaughter for human consumption must really only be undertaken under veterinary guidance. You must consider whether the pig is fit to travel, will the carcase be fit for human consumption, and is the animal suitable for treatment? If at all unsure you must discuss this with your veterinary surgeon. It would be wise to have a 'standard operating procedure', and a checklist agreed for these situations with your veterinary surgeon. There are considered to be four possible outcomes for a casualty pig. The first would be to treat it under veterinary advice, and euthanase it promptly and humanely if it does not respond to treatment: current thinking is that it should respond within five days. The second possibility is that the pig can be sent for casualty slaughter if it is suitable for transport and slaughter in the nearest suitable slaughterhouse. It must be accompanied by an owner's written declaration (FCI). The third outcome is immediate euthanasia on farm where there is no hope of treatment success. The fourth outcome would be to decide to sell to normal slaughter as appropriate if the ailment is considered minor. The 2006 transport regulations state that 'animals may be considered fit for transport if they are slightly injured or ill and transport will not cause additional suffering'.

Summary of points relating to casualty slaughter

- You are ultimately responsible for the welfare of your animals
- Never attempt to kill a pig without suitable training
- The method must render the pig unconscious immediately
- Never allow an unconscious pig to regain consciousness
- It is an offence to keep alive an animal that is suffering (pain or distress) when there is no realistic prospect of recovery
- Regardless of all regulations and advice, in an absolute emergency, if the usual method of euthanasia is unavailable, any method may be used to kill a pig so long as it renders it immediately unconscious
- All methods of killing pigs are potentially dangerous to humans (and other livestock), and due diligence to safety must be shown
- Ignorance of the law is no excuse….

(Adapted from the Pig Veterinary Society – *The Casualty Pig* Interim update pdf April 2013.)

Transport

Transport is stressful for pigs, particularly when animals are mixed during loading and transit. The Cambac Pig Marketing Group and JMA Research Project in the 1980s into the transport of pigs prior to slaughter yielded information that led to both improved animal welfare and economic performance. Stocking rates on livestock lorries were found to have a big influence on live-weight losses, which varied between 2 and a staggering 10 per cent. Densely stocked pigs lost weight in each of six trials. The time of day also influenced the number of deaths, afternoon deliveries having the highest mortality rate. Drivers also influenced the number of deaths, which would suggest that driving style is important. Careful handling of pigs is vital. Loading and unloading lorries and trailers from purpose-built loading bays and ramps is now an essential aspect of modern pig management.

Legislation and directives controlling the maximum length of time animals can be transported are in force and must be adhered to. Since April 2008, everybody hauling (transporting) pigs should have a Certificate of Competence in Animal Transport. This includes a written test designed for practical people. The driver of the vehicle is responsible for the animals when they are being transported.

FURTHER INFORMATION

www.thepigsite.com/diseaseinfo/
www.bpex.org.uk/2ts/health/FarmHealth/
www.pighealth.org.uk/phip/home.eb
www.bpex.org.uk/2TS/health/Bphs/default.aspx
www.porktraining.org/
'Pig Health and Welfare Council Annual Reports' via www.bpex.
org.uk
National Animal Disease Information Service: www.nadis.org.uk/
livestock/pigs.aspx

www.thepigsite.com/diseaseinfo/41/erysipelas

NOTIFIABLE DISEASES: KNOW THE SIGNS AND WHAT ACTION TO TAKE IF THERE IS A SUSPECTED CASE:
Links:

African Swine Fever (is also carried by 'soft ticks' (Ornithodorus))
www.defra.gov.uk/animal-diseases/a-z/african-swine-fever/

scotland.gov.uk/Topics/farmingrural/Agriculture/animal-welfare/Diseases/disease/african/signs

Swine Fever (CSF)
www.defra.gov.uk/ahvla-en/disease-control/notifiable/csf/
www.scotland.gov.uk/Topics/farmingrural/Agriculture/animal-welfare/Diseases/disease/fever/signs

Foot and mouth disease (affects cloven hoofed animals)
www.defra.gov.uk/ahvla-en/disease-control/notifiable/fmd/
www.scotland.gov.uk/Topics/farmingrural/Agriculture/animal-welfare/Diseases/disease/foot

Anthrax, Aujeszky's disease, Rabies, Swine vesicular disease, etc.
www.defra.gov.uk/ahvla-en/disease-control/notifiable/

10

Showing and Carcase Competitions

Showing live pigs was once the most effective marketing tool for the traditional pedigree breeder. This marketing role continues, but you should also see showing as an enjoyable and thoroughly rewarding exercise. Of course, the considerable amount of work involved is no less than it was in years gone by.

The beginner should attend some local and national events prior to starting out in the show ring. Talking to experienced showmen will be a big help, as they are almost certainly all enthusiasts and many are also highly professional in their approach. At the same time, you should take the opportunity to study the show schedule and obtain copies of the 'standards of excellence' produced by the relevant breed councils.

Start off by showing younger stock, in the six- to twelve-month age group. These should be raised as a group and not as individuals: pigs are gregarious animals, and as young pig classes require groups, they should come from the same pen. Do not forget that most strange pigs will need some time to get to know each other before you dare take them to a show as a group.

Carcase competitions are often run at local and county shows. Contact your abattoir, and make sure you have the local show catalogues in order to plan ahead. The rare breeds will need to be fed on a tight ration to get back fats to match the modern hybrids which will also compete. Carcase competitions are very educational, and they provide an excellent opportunity to discuss your pigs with butchers and other pig producers. A good show pig should also make a good carcase: the two go hand in hand.

Before you can even start thinking about going to a show, you must ensure that all pig movement regulations can be complied with. All pigs moved on to and off your unit must have the appropriate animal movements documentation and notifications. Under certain circumstances there will be a statutory limit (for example, a twenty days' standstill), during which time movement of pigs off your unit will be prohibited. There is an exemption for premises licensed under the Animal Gatherings (England) Order 2010 for a sale, show or exhibition (*see* www.gov.uk PDFs).

Now the work can begin. Make sure you enter the show in time, and have full details recorded well ahead of time. Select your animals on the basis of conformation, breed type, health, physical characteristics and gait. Do not forget to keep group sizes small, and avoid fights because unsightly scratches and bruises will lose you many points. Feed the pigs carefully and avoid digestive upsets (scours). Ensure that they are free of all internal and external parasites.

Practise walking your pigs using pig bats and boards. 'Prizes are won at home', so the old saying goes, and you should take plenty of time to exercise your pig in a simulated show ring: it will pay dividends. At the show you will have to keep the pig walking unless the judge or steward tells you to stop; the pig must do as you want, and you should learn to drive it from both sides.

Begin your final preparations by washing the pigs using warm (but not hot) water and green soap or gentle animal shampoo. Dry them with ground sawdust, and oil them with good quality products, especially vegetable oils. Sows and boars do not always enjoy a wash, and it may be worthwhile washing them in a purpose-built metal crate or an adapted farrowing crate.

Once at the show take great care if it is sunny, especially if there is no tent cover. Clean pigs will suffer from sunburn much more rapidly than dirty ones. Bed them up with plenty of good quality, clean wheat straw. Barley straw is fine in itself, but tends to have lots of awns, which will get into eyes and ears. Rub in plenty of wood flour, and cover the pigs' backs to keep them clean until just before you enter the ring; then brush it off and give the pigs a last once-over. However, do not use wood flour on Large Blacks because it is impossible to clean it off properly – rather, oil them after washing.

Get into the ring as soon as the steward calls your class. This allows the judge to take a good look at your pig first – though be careful not to get in their way. And make sure you are as well turned out as the pig!

Equipment needed includes buckets, a calor gas boiler, a churn for water, and your show box (keep your rosettes on the inside lid), which should contain two brushes (scrub and dry), a sponge, a thick towelling cloth, a bag of wood flour or oil if you have black pigs, a pig board, pig bats, a hammer, nails, string (baler twine),

Young man showing.

Anthony Mosley

embrocation lotion for stiff joints and a first aid box. Your own attire should include a clean, pressed white coat, clean wellington boots, and waterproofs for a rainy day. Do not forget your paperwork and lorry or car exhibitor's pass.

In hot weather you should travel early with the pigs penned securely, head to tail with straw sacks at the tail end. Do not unload until you have bedded up the pen. Take plenty of straw and a tarpaulin sheet to protect the pigs from sun, wind and rain, if necessary. Take care and time when loading and unloading.

Showing involves a great deal of hard work, but it can be very rewarding if you are enthusiastic and take it seriously. It is not for everyone, but those who perform this shop window task for agriculture seem to enjoy themselves thoroughly – and long may they continue to do so.

FURTHER INFORMATION

Essential and useful information concerning showing and judging:
www.britishpigs.org.uk/shows.htm
www.nfyfc.org.uk/CompetitionsResources/ – see 'Stockjudging guide –
finished pig and pig carcase.
Animal movement regulations and procedures:
www.gov.uk/government/uploads/.../annexa-c-090713.pdf and
www.gov.uk/.../uploads/.../pb13647-new-pig-keepers-guide.
pdf

— 11 —

Future Developments

Scientific developments over the past twenty-five years since the first editions were published have ensured the success and even the very survival of the pig industry in its current form. Advances in breeding, nutrition, technology and, most important of all, animal health and the control of diseases, have all been exceptional, and this trend will undoubtedly continue. The development of effective vaccines has been pivotal in ensuring the financial survival of a large proportion of the pig herds operating across the globe. In 2013, approaching two-thirds of the national herds in many countries are known to be infected with PRRSv. The development of new vaccine resources continues, and will undoubtedly help to maintain a good degree of control over this devastating disease. Biosecurity systems will also play an increasingly important role at an international, national, local and on-farm level. On-farm, this is already being aided by virucidal disinfectants that operate more effectively at low and even sub-zero temperatures.

New diseases are constantly emerging, and the risk of one or other of the notifiable diseases, such as African swine fever, classical swine fever or foot and mouth disease crossing our shores, is a constant threat. International and national biosecurity will have to be continually improved to help ensure our national herds remain free of these devastating diseases, which have the potential to destroy a country's ability to trade in live breeding stock and meat exports for many months and sometimes years afterwards.

The pig meat industry will continue to become even more globalized, with a high proportion of the pig carcase and the 'fifth quarter' – the liver and other internal organs – destined for export rather than home consumption, such as it already is in countries like the UK that are not self-sufficient (2013). This will continue to develop as an important source of income for the pig meat industry, which in turn has a direct effect on the price that can be paid for the finished pig in each country.

There has been a many-fold increase in the number of people keeping pigs on a small scale producing for niche markets, simply as a hobby, or even as pets. This increases the risk of someone feeding these pigs illegally on human food waste, which can potentially carry and pass on one of the notifiable diseases mentioned above. Foot and mouth is wind spread, and as a veterinary colleague describes it: 'A single blister bursting on an infected pig's snout can potentially infect 10,000 other cloven-footed animals downwind for 30 or 40 kilometres.' Biosecurity really does begin at home.

Welfare issues will continue to require our attention. The quest for 'freedom farrowing' on indoor units across the globe must address the mortality rate of the piglets as well as improving sow welfare. High performance breeding sows rearing twelve or thirteen piglets or more per litter will always need top class management and supervision to keep piglet mortality rates within single figures. The move to heavier slaughter weights in the UK, and the banning of castration in other countries, poses the risk of boars reaching sexual maturity before slaughter and of increased fighting and aggression. These are all examples of where a highly desirable welfare improvement at one stage of the pig's life can effect a reduction in welfare standards at another. These are all challenges we will always face, and we must strive for practical solutions. Maintaining high welfare is a constant and continuing issue, and should be seen as the basis of good pig keeping.

In 2013, about 40 per cent of the UK pig breeding herd is based on outdoor pig production up to weaning and often through until the piglets are 35kg. This potential trend was correctly predicted in the first editions. This has clearly occurred because of production economic factors and the developments discussed earlier. This sector currently has a high proportion of approved outdoor breeding herds supported in the marketing of their pigs through membership of welfare schemes such as RSPCA Freedom Foods. This provides improved marketing opportunities for meat from outdoor-born pigs retailed under the Freedom Foods logo. Similarly, the Red Tractor Scheme, with an increased emphasis on 'real welfare', is also increasingly important to all sectors of the UK pig industry.

The problem for outdoor production will be in keeping its production costs down and maintaining a favourable price differential in face of competition from indoor production systems at home and abroad. Achieving and maintaining an increase in the number of piglets per sow per year will always be more challenging on an outdoor unit. The need for a niche product price premium will become even more important when the price differential increases between outdoor born pigs and imported or UK pig meat produced indoors.

The high reliance on straw-bedded systems in the UK forms the basis for many of the welfare-based assurance schemes and also organic production. The future supply of good quality straw bedding is potentially threatened by the development of straw-burning electricity generating power stations. There is considered to be enough scope to source lower quality straw for burning currently chopped and ploughed in immediately after harvest. It will be important for farming industry representatives and the authorities to monitor this closely, as the risk is there for inadequate supplies and increased prices. Straw already costs around £60 (2013) per sow per year on outdoor units, compared to an average £18 on a typical indoor unit (where applicable).

The pig industry must become an early adopter of new technology and apply science to develop practical solutions to animal health, welfare, production economics, sustainability and all the various other challenges facing the industry. Collecting information and using it effectively in real-time should form the basis of how we work at every level in pig production. This also applies to how we react as pig keepers and collectively to food scares and health scares that can have a direct impact on our enterprises, however large or small. It would be desirable to expect every secondary school leaver to have read *Bad Science* by Ben Goldacre (Harper Collins 2008), so that everyone has a fighting chance of spotting inaccurate, contradictory and sometimes completely misleading information presented to us as hard facts. We should also ensure that those representing our particular interests continue to work effectively from a sound and credible base.

Like many other types of farmer, pig farmers are an ageing group, and the concern remains relating to the recruitment of young people into the pig industry. There are some excellent careers on-farm in the pig industry, as well as in the crucial roles carried out by veterinarians, nutritionists, geneticists, pig housing, technology and pig business specialists.

The pig meat supply chain has developed positively over the past years, and it is hoped that the consumer will have trust and confidence in the pig meat products they are purchasing. This will be achieved through an improved transparency of the origins, welfare, health and quality of the pigs at all stages in the production process. High health and welfare standards are required, and it is hoped that the pig meat supply chain will reward those who produce to these standards sufficiently well to maintain the level of investment required for the future of both large and small scale pig keeping.

The 'June Returns' for 2012 are reported by DEFRA to show that there are 11,000 commercial farms keeping pigs. This is an increase over the 2011 figures. The structure of the pig industry is interesting when we consider that more than 80 per cent of all pigs are kept on holdings with more than 1,000 head (all age groups). This translates into 1,360 units holding 80 per cent of all pigs. The picture for breeding pigs shows 90 per cent of sows kept on 900 holdings with more than 100 sows. These 900 holdings averaged 440 sows. This means that 20 per cent of all pigs and 10 per cent of UK sows are kept on close to 10,000 smaller-scale production units. These pig keepers will range in size from a few pigs up to 100 sows or 1,000 pigs in total. These smaller scale businesses appear to be increasing in number, and this trend may well continue.

The 'food scares' over the past few decades have undoubtedly created a desire for 'provenance' and locally produced food. Testing where meat comes from will probably become increasingly important, and can be carried out very effectively using SIRA tests (Stable Isotope Ratio Analysis). Consumers will always be influenced by price, but retail marketing analysts also talk about the importance of the 'non-price offer' – referring to the consumer's desire to know where the food comes from. This trend underlines the importance of 'Red Tractor' and 'Freedom Foods' recognition of this 'non-price offer' across the whole range of pig meat products. This also applies to the potential for an increase in small-scale, locally produced pig meat products from farms close to and often known by the consumer.

Financial challenges will always remain for all pig keepers, with the achievement of good sale returns from high welfare quality products, along with feeding and rearing their pigs economically remaining top priorities.

Appendix I
Records

Essential records include those that must be kept for legal or official reasons. These include animal movement records, medicines records, pedigree records and financial records for tax and VAT. These should be seen as routine records, and apart from minor modifications, they are of a standard format and can increasingly be carried out online or via mobile applications.

An essential task for all pig businesses, large or small, is the choice, setting up and operation of production and performance recording schemes.

The breeding herd ideally demands individual sow and boar recording, whilst the weaner, grower and finisher herds may only require total pig numbers, feed use and growth rates to be measured. There are a number of commercial recording schemes available such as Agrosoft and PigCom. Bureau-based systems such as Pig-Plan involve completing periodic reports giving stock numbers, feed use, carcase and financial details. The feedback varies from comprehensive analyses of performance, measured in a numeric form, to ones that include useful graphical presentation. The PigPlan scheme can also include individual sow and boar monitoring, where cards showing sow performance are returned each time an event is recorded for her. In schemes such as PigPlan and Agrosoft it is possible to compare performance between herds or similar types of herd.

Computer-based pig-recording programs are also popular. These programs vary in their initial cost and potential for analysis. Users of on-farm computers find the action lists of considerable help in planning their work. These also produce a detailed analysis, on demand, similar to the bureau-based systems. Data input can involve mobile technology as well as keyboard input. These schemes will usually supply recording cards or sheets.

In practice, it would be wise to keep the following minimum production records in addition to sow cards and insemination/service register records:

- A desk diary for basic information, for example pigs sold
- A barn book to record weights of feed deliveries and stock control
- A pig count stock control sheet, including weights of weaners and finishing pigs where applicable

The weaner grower or finisher herds will require the following paper or electronic records:

- Identity of individual animals or, more commonly, groups, in pens
- Date of entering feeder/finishing unit or date when, say, 25kg was reached
- Weight at entry
- Date sold off the farm
- Weight at date of sale
- Carcase details**

* Health records – this should include a visitors' book with full contact details. This will be required if there is a major disease outbreak to allow the authorities to take appropriate action.

**Computers allow rapid analysis of carcase record sheets, as described in Chapter 7. Recording is very much concerned with monitoring production in a pig herd. You can then set and revise targets, investigate shortfalls and take action. This should lead you to a more easily managed and efficient pig business.

Movement of Animals records are complex and it is a legal requirement to maintain and operate these records and procedures correctly. (*See* Chapter 2 for some examples current in 2013.) Local Trading Standards will provide advice and electronic or paper-based record pages/book. For example, *see* www.cambridgeshire.gov.uk/business/trading/agriculture/farm.htm.

The same applies to recording veterinary medicines. A veterinary medicine record can be downloaded in pdf format. *See also*: www.vmd.defra.gov.uk/pdf/vmgn/VMGNote14.pdf
Veterinary Medicines Guidance Note No. 14 (correct 09/2013).

Setting and Monitoring Targets

An example of an Excel graph produced to give live-weight targets for an individual herd. This also shows a minimum weight for age. In this example the range is set at fourteen to twenty days between the target and minimum. In this case the target is to finish pigs to 100kg by twenty-one weeks of age (147 days), and a minimum of about twenty-three to twenty-four weeks (161 to 168 days). This would correspond to daily gains from eleven to twelve weeks to 100kg of 928g per day (Target) and 774g per day minimum.

This requires an accurate ability to know the age of pigs or at least batches/pens of pigs. Some farms use different coloured ear tags or an ear-notch system to ensure accurate age identification.

Realistic targets can be set, together with the supplier of the breeding stock, nutritionists and veterinarians.

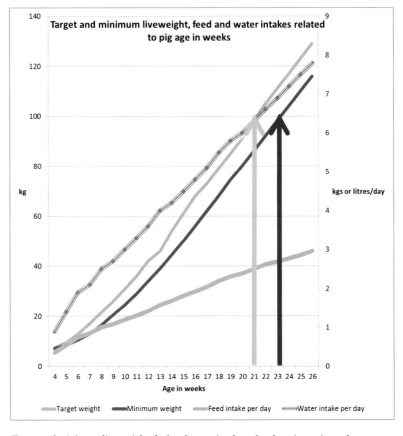

Target and minimum live-weight, feed and water intakes related to pig age in weeks.

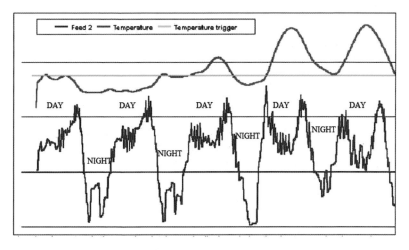

| Feed 2 | Temperature | Temperature trigger |

Feed intake and the temperature effect. NICK BIRD, FARMEX, 2001

Recording information and retrieving information and data can now be carried out using mobile hand held devices. Wireless internet allows direct access to information, advice and the ability to complete animal movement documentation on line. This can also link in to remote sensing data, such as the feed or water consumption data illustrated above.

219

A laminated poster-sized version of this target-setting approach works well when placed close to the weighing area, or at least on the wall of the pig unit office for all to see.

Feed and water intakes are also a useful addition, and these can be monitored much more easily than in the past using electronic recording.

The graph on page 219 illustrates the feed (and water) intake recorded using a Farmex system which is linked to the internet. The five days show how temperature affects pig feed intake patterns. When the ambient house temperature is maintained below the desired maximum the pigs begin to feed in the morning and increase intake gradually through the day, and consume little during the early hours of the morning. As soon as the ambient temperatures goes above the 'trigger' value they move towards feeding more during the cooler early morning and evening periods, and eat more throughout the cooler night. This also has clear implications where pigs do not have a choice of when they eat.

Remote monitoring of all aspects of the pig's environment is now possible and offers opportunities to modify management to improve both pig behaviour and welfare, along with maintaining economic feed use, health and growth rates.

Opposite is a good example of a computer-based sow record of an individual sow achieving close to the UK indoor herd (2013) average number of piglets reared per year. This can be viewed on screen or printed out as required. This sow has already reared sixty-eight piglets to weaning from seven litters. She returned to service on her fifth parity, with a farrowing interval of 167 days compared to about 146 days for the other six parities. She lost twenty-one days because she failed to conceive. Her overall farrowing rate was six out of seven from each post-weaning mating, or better said 86 per cent. This is the minimum target we should aim for, because each day the sow loses will cost at least £2 (2013 costs) or £42 for each sow failing to conceive. These days lost are known as 'empty days'.

This is an example of how we can begin to interpret our sow records. Computer-based recording systems also produce a whole range of useful analysis options, allowing the herd's staff to monitor and modify management, along with the herd veterinarian, nutritionist or pig specialist adviser. Keeping good records is an essential task, and using the information derived from them is absolutely invaluable in a herd of any size.

L819

Tattoo /
Date In 10-Jan-06 ()
D.O.B.

Sire
Dam
Transponder

Farm **3 WEEK BATCH**

Breed **OWN**

Parity **8**

21-May

	Service Date	Day	Boar Tag	Breed of Litter	3 Week Date	115 Days
1	26-Jan-09	4	4013		16-Feb-09	21-May
2						
3						

Previous Litters

Pty	Fint	Gest	D.O.B.	Live	Dead	Mmfd	Wt	On	Off	No.	Age	Wt	Comment
1		117	10/07/06	9	0	0	0	0	0	7	24	56	
2	144	115	01/12/06	12	0	0	0	0	0	10	27	80	
3	147	116	27/04/07	14	0	0	0	0	0	8	27	64	
4	147	116	21/09/07	12	2	0	0	0	0	11	27	88	
5	167	115	06/03/08	13	1	0	0	0	0	11	28	88	
6	149	117	02/08/08	11	0	0	0	0	0	9	26	72	
7	147	116	27/12/08	8	0	1	0	0	0	12	26	96	
Av.	150	116		11.3	0.4	0.1	0.0 0.00	0.0	0.0	9.7	26.4	80.0 1.18	Live/Sow/Year 27.4 Wean/Sow/Year 23.8

Header spanning: Numbers Born (Live, Dead, Mmfd, Wt), Fostering (On, Off), Weaning (No., Age, Wt)

Current Litter

D.O.B.	Male	Female	Dead	Mmfd	Wt	On	Off	Weaned	Wean Wt	Comment

Piglet Deaths

Pty	Location	Total	Laid On	Low Viab.	Starvatn	Scour	Savaged	Defects	Other
1		1	1	0	0	0	0	0	0
2		2	0	1	1	0	0	0	0
3		3	3	0	0	0	0	0	0
4		0	0	0	0	0	0	0	0
5		4	4	0	0	0	0	0	0
6		2	2	0	0	0	0	0	0
7	44	0	0	0	0	0	0	0	0
Total		12.0	10.0	1.0	1.0	0.0	0.0	0.0	0.0
% of Piglet Mortality		100.0	83.3	8.3	8.3	0.0	0.0	0.0	0.0
% of Born Live		15.2	12.7	1.3	1.3	0.0	0.0	0.0	0.0

Sow Treatments

Date	Condition	Drug	Doses	Quantity
26-Dec-08	Assist Farrowing	Planate	1	2
27-Dec-08	Assist Farrowing	Reprocine	1	1

ACMC Pig Herd Management System - www.pigcom.co.uk.

First 10 days (All sows/Gilts)

Day	kg	Fed
1	2.5	
2	3.0	
3	3.5	
4	4.0	
5	4.5	
6	5.0	
7	5.5	
8	6.0	
9	6.5	
10	7.0	

Sow Identification

Total Fed:

Date Farrowed (Day 1)

NOTES:

Gilt <10 piglets / Sow <9 piglets

Day	kg	Fed
11	7.0	
12	7.0	
13	7.5	
14	7.5	
15	8.0	
16	8.0	
17	8.5	
18	8.5	
19	9.0	
20	9.0	
21	9.5	
22	9.5	
23	9.5	
24	9.5	
25	9.5	
26	9.5	
27	9.5	

Gilt 10 piglets / Sow 9 piglets

Day	kg	Fed
11	7.5	
12	7.5	
13	8.0	
14	8.0	
15	8.5	
16	8.5	
17	9.0	
18	9.0	
19	9.5	
20	9.5	
21	10.0	
22	10.0	
23	10.0	
24	10.0	
25	10.0	
26	10.0	
27	10.0	

Gilt 11 piglets / Sow 10 piglets

Day	kg	Fed
11	7.5	
12	8.0	
13	8.5	
14	8.5	
15	9.0	
16	9.0	
17	9.5	
18	9.5	
19	10.0	
20	10.0	
21	10.5	
22	10.5	
23	10.5	
24	10.5	
25	10.5	
26	10.5	
27	10.5	

Gilt 12 piglets / Sow 11 piglets

Day	kg	Fed
11	7.5	
12	8.0	
13	8.5	
14	9.0	
15	9.5	
16	9.5	
17	10.0	
18	10.0	
19	10.5	
20	10.5	
21	11.0	
22	11.0	
23	11.0	
24	11.0	
25	11.0	
26	11.0	
27	11.0	

Gilt 13 piglets / Sow 12 piglets

Day	kg	Fed
11	7.5	
12	8.0	
13	8.5	
14	9.0	
15	9.5	
16	10.0	
17	10.5	
18	10.5	
19	11.0	
20	11.0	
21	11.5	
22	11.5	
23	11.5	
24	11.5	
25	11.5	
26	11.5	
27	11.5	

Note: This can be copied to use as a recording sheet for each sow. It can also be downloaded from www.carrsconsulting.com/thepig/health-farm/productionmgt/farrowing/feed/stotfold.PDF. *See* Chapter 8, Sow and Gilt Management – Stotfold Scale lactation feed intake graph.

Appendix II
Laws, Regulations and Assurance Schemes

There are numerous laws and regulations applicable to pig farming, pig keepers and those who care for the animals, transport them, and at markets and abattoirs. Examples of these are listed below, with suggested web-site links where detailed current information can be obtained. The UK has devolved governments in Northern Ireland, Scotland and Wales, whilst England is currently governed by the laws made by the British Government in Westminster. Local authorities will also have some control, especially in respect to planning regulations. Existing pig keepers and those planning to keep pigs must make sure they are compliant with the current laws and regulations that apply to their situation. This is an increasingly complex issue, and the following are important examples of some of the main areas demanding full compliance.

A useful place to begin can be found on the following web site (all web links as per 2013): www.gov.uk/browse/business/farming.

Animal Welfare

The United Kingdom was the first country in the world to implement laws protecting animals. In 1822 an Act to Prevent the Cruel and Improper Treatment of Cattle was passed by Parliament. The first general animal protection law, called the Protection of Animals Act, was introduced in 1911 and has been updated several times since.

The Animal Welfare Act, an overhaul of pet abuse laws replacing the Protection of Animals Act, came into force in England and Wales in 2007.

Farm animals are included under the Animal Welfare Act and, more specifically, the Welfare of Farmed Animals (England) Regulations 2007. Welfare codes have been created for most animals that are farmed commercially in the UK. These can be downloaded from the DEFRA website.

Europe

Council Directive 2001/88/EC and Commission Directive 2001/93/ EC, laid down minimum standards for the welfare of pigs. In 2008 the Commission replaced both of these directives with council directive 2008/120/EC. The UK was already compliant in most respects, and this directive also brought in the regulation banning the keeping of gestating sows in confined sow stalls after the first four weeks of gestation. All EU countries had to comply by 1 January 2013. The UK had already enforced stricter rules more than a decade previously, which demanded that all gestating sows are kept in groups in non-confinement systems immediately after weaning through to their entry into the farrowing accommodation for their next farrowing.

Useful website links:

- www.gov.uk/pig-welfare-regulations: a comprehensive guide and links for further information, including the Welfare Codes for Pigs which should be downloaded and put on display
- www.rspca.org.uk – also have their own codes (*see also* 'Freedom Foods assurance scheme below).
- www.bbc.co.uk/ethics/animals/defending/legislation_1.shtml

The Animal Health and Veterinary Laboratories Agency (AHVLA) is responsible for enforcement of pig welfare legislation in England and carries out welfare inspections on farms to check that the legislation and the welfare codes are being followed. The RSPCA also have a legal role in enforcing animal welfare laws.

Health and Disease

This includes the control of animal movement (*see* Chapter 2 for some detailed information relating to the rules, regulations and procedures relating to animal movement and the need for premises that keep pigs – even 'Micro' pigs – to be registered). The important areas for the pig keeper to be aware of and comply with are those involving health and disease monitoring, prevention and control; plus pig identification, registration and movement.

Useful website links:

- www.gov.uk/pig-health-disease-monitoring-prevention-and-control
- www.gov.uk/pigs-identification-registration-and-movement
- www.nadis.org.uk/livestock/pigs.aspx -National Animal Disease Information Service
- www.defra.gov.uk/ahvla-en/disease-control/abp/fallen-stock-faq/ AHLVA information regarding responsibility for fallen stock (carcases of dead farm animals). Also:
- www.legislation.gov.uk/uksi/2011/881/contents/made The Animal By-Products (Enforcement) (England) Regulations 2011

Environmental

Very strict environmental regulations apply to farming, just as it does to industry. Pig farmers with more than a specified number of pigs on one location are subject to regular costly environmental inspections and regulations. Amongst others, the minimum storage period capacity for pig slurry and when it can be spread on the land are defined and must be adhered to. The following website links and pdf downloads will provide the up-to-date information from the Environment Agency:

- www.environment-agency.gov.uk/business/sectors/32795.aspx
- www.environment-agency.gov.uk/static/documents/Business/ippc_comply_0406_1397535.pdf
- www.doeni.gov.uk/niea/standardfarmingrulesv3pigrearing09.pdf (Northern Ireland)

Pet Pigs and 'Micro' Pigs

- www.defra.gov.uk/ahvla-en/files/pub-pigs-micro-pet.pdf
- www.tradingstandards.gov.uk/cgi-bin/glos/con1item.cgi?file...1001...
- www.rspca.org.uk › ... › Our pets › Farm animals as pets and PDF @Advice to Owners of Pet Pigs and 'Micro' Pigs
- www.scotland.gov.uk/Topics/farmingrural/Agriculture/animal-welfare/IDtraceability/pig
  wales.gov.uk/topics/environmentcountryside/ahw/farmanimaltracing/pigkeepersguidance/?lang=en

Planning Controls Affecting Pig Producers

Planning controls will vary over time along with other codes, rules and statutory regulations. It is essential to obtain expert advice when planning any development relating to pig production. Plans for an intensive pig unit may require an environmental impact assessment and cross compliance. Detailed explanations of the procedures are available at:

- www.gov.uk/developing-farmland-regulations-on-land-use#environmental-impact-assessment-and-cross-compliance

The following PDF download provides further details:

- adlib.everysite.co.uk/resources/000/020/065/planning-guide.pdf
  also:
- www.bpex.org.uk/downloads/295527/283961/Environmental%20Management%20for%20Healthy%20Pig%20Production.pdf

Health and Safety

The Health and Safety at Work Act and the Control of Substances Hazardous to Health (COSHH) Regulations apply on the pig unit. Information and guidance can be obtained from the Health and Safety Executive (HSE) and HSEI (Northern Ireland).

Organic Production

Selling produce with an organic label is only possible with full compliance with an approved organic control body such as the 'Soil Association':

- www.soilassociation.org and www.soilassociation.org/scotland
- www.assurewel.org/pigs

Other Assurance Schemes (examples)

Freedom Food – the RSPCA-monitored scheme based on the RSPCA Welfare Standards:

- www.freedomfood.co.uk/industry/rspca-welfare-standards

Red Tractor Assurance for Farms – Pig Scheme:

- assurance.redtractor.org.uk/rtassurance/farm/pigs/pg_
  about.eb

Wild Boar Farming

Wild boar are covered by the 'Dangerous Wild Animals Act 1976 (Modification) Order 1984' and a licence is required to keep the animals.* This also applies to domestic pig × wild boar hybrids, providing one of the parents is a wild boar. Licensing laws may change in the future. A DEFRA commissioned report on the effectiveness of the Act recommended farmed wild boar to be removed from the Act. (Source: www.britishwildboar.org.uk/index.htm?breeding.htm)

Further information on feral wild boar in Britain:

- www.basc.org.uk/en/departments/deer-management/
  wild-boar/
- www.wild-boar.org.uk/ (useful information on biology and
  behaviour)
- www.naturalengland.org.uk/Images/wildboarstatusImpact
  management_tcm6-4512.pdf (status, impact and management
  of feral wild boar in England)

Approved and suitable perimeter fencing and gateway security are required to keep farmed wild boar. In central Europe outdoor pig units are often required to erect similar fencing to keep the roving wild boar population away from domestic outdoor and indoor pigs and their feed.

---

* From the local authority.

Useful Addresses

All types: www.pig-guide.com

AI CENTRES

Pedigree pigs and rare breeds:
www.britishpigs.org.uk/aisemen.htm
Deerpark Pedigree Pigs, JJ Genetics, Glenmarshall Sires, Elite Sires

BPEX AI Standards:
www.bpex.org.uk/downloads/300829/298983/KT%20Bulletin%208%20-%20
AI%20Standard.pdf
The following breeding companies participated in the initial AI Quality Standards
scheme and provide commercial AI services:
ACMC, Hermitage Seaborough, JSR, PIC and Rattlerow Farms.

Breeding pigs and AI:
ACMC: www.acmc.co.uk
Hermitage Seaborough: www.hermitage.ie/
JSR Genetics: www.jsrgenetics.com/
PIC UK: www.pic.com/uk
Rattlerow Farms Ltd: www.rattlerow.co.uk/

Independent Breeders and Pedigree pigs:
www.britishpigs.org.uk/ and for each breed:
www.britishpigs.org.uk/breedlist.htm
Rare Breeds Survival Trust https://www.rbst.org.uk/
https://www.rbst.org.uk/watchlist.pdf

GOVERNMENT ORGANIZATIONS AND AGENCIES

AHLVA www.defra.gov.uk/ahvla-en/(Animal Health)
BPEX www.bpex.org.uk/(AHDB)
DEFRA https://www.gov.uk/defra (General)
Environment Agency www.environment-agency.gov.uk/
Fallen Stock www.nfsco.co.uk/
Local Government Association www.local.gov.uk/
Trading Standards www.tradingstandards.gov.uk/

FARMING TRADE AND OTHER ORGANIZATIONS

BPA www.britishpigs.org.uk/
NFU www.nfuonline.com/home/
NPA www.npa-uk.org.uk/
LIPS (Ladies in Pigs) www.ladiesinpigs.co.uk/
LovePork www.lovepork.co.uk/love-pigs/

HEALTH AND WELFARE

BVA www.bva.co.uk
eAML2 (electronic movement services) www.eaml2.org.uk/
Humane Slaughter Association www.hsa.org.uk
NADIS www.nadis.org.uk/
Pig Veterinary Society www.pvs.org.uk
RSPCA and Freedom Foods www.rspca.org.uk/freedomfood and www.freedom-food.co.uk
Soil Association www.soilassociation.org (organic standards and welfare standards)
Pig Health Improvement Project www.pighealth.org.uk

PIG CAREERS

Pig Careers.org.uk - For details of career opportunities in the British Pig Industry www.pigcareers.org.uk/
Continuing Professional Development (CPD) and Pig Industry Professional Register https://www.pipr.org.uk/
See also: Young NPA at www.npa-uk.org.uk/

Examples of commercial pig feed suppliers:
ABN - www.abn.co.uk/
BOCM Pauls - www.bocmpauls.co.uk/
For specialist and starter diets and others see: www.pig-guide.com **under 'Feeding'**

Examples of specialist feed suppliers for smallholders:
Farmgate Feeds: www.farmgatefeeds.co.uk/
W & H Mariage and Sons Ltd: www.marriagefeeds.co.uk
The Smallholder Range: www.smallholderfeed.co.uk/
Countrywide: www.countrywidefarmers.co.uk

PET PIGS

The British KuneKune Pig Society for Kunekune pig:
www.britishkunekunesociety.org.uk /
www.countrywidefarmers.co.uk/.../Content.ice?...GuidesHowToChooseK...
Vietnamese Pot Bellied and Kunekune: www.pigs.org/article.asp?article_id=3

Chapter References

Chapter 2:
* Those starting with pigs for the first time can download the government pdf publication 'Guide for Pig Keepers': https://www.gov.uk/government/publications/a-guide-for-pig-keepers
This covers aspects such as the current procedures for registering the holding, identification of pigs, registration and on-farm records for pigs.

* Whether you keep one pig as a pet or you run a commercial herd, you need to be registered with the Department for Environment, Food and Rural Affairs (Defra). To view the eAML2 electronic movement licence details go to the following web sites:
www.britishpigs.org.uk/eaml2_intro.htm
www.countrywidefarmers.co.uk/pws/pdf/how_to_guides/How_to_Smallholder_choose_and_keep_pigs.pdf

* Breeds at Risk register: see: archive.defra.gov.uk/foodfarm/farmanimal/diseases/atoz/fmd/about/riskreg.htm
and;www.accidentalsmallholder.net/forum/index.php?topic=30102.0

Chapter 3:
* Anyone obtaining waste milk, milk products or white water to feed to their pigs would need to register with Defra for this purpose, although in the case of milk products, this would only be necessary it they contained more than 80 per cent milk. Details on how to register are available from either the Defra helpline (08459 33 55 77) or the internet archive.defra.gov.uk/foodfarm/farmanimal/movements/pigs/documents/new_owner_guide.pdf   correct   as at   4/2013   and   www.defra.gov.uk/ahvla-en/disease-control/abp/food-feed-businesses/disposal-treat-use-milk-products/ correct as at 10/2013.

* The UK organic pig producer must ensure that the animals only receive feeds that contain feed ingredients and additives as approved by the Soil Association. The Newcastle University Handbook on raw materials for organic pigs is also a useful reference; it is available from the BPA website in pdf format: www.britishpigs.org.uk/Newcastle_handbook_of_raw_materials.pdf

* **Information on feed and nutrition in pig health:** www.thepigsite.com/pighealth/article/512/the-role-of-amino-acids and other feed components.

Chapter 4:
* Area requirements for pigs: *see also* https://www.gov.uk/pig-welfare-regulations
* Housing systems: Finrone Systems Ltd: *WWW.**FINRONESYSTEMS**.COM*

Chapter 5:
* The AI process: access pdf leaflets and training videos at www.bpex.org.uk or practicalpig.bpex.org.uk.
* Pedigree pig breeders can obtain details of AI centres from www.britishpigs.org.uk/aisemen.htm.
* For details of the BPEX AI Quality Standard, refer to: www.bpex.org.uk/downloads/300829/298983/KT%20Bulletin%208%20-%20AI%20Standard.pdf

Chapter 7:
* The BPEX calculator service: available at www.bpex.org.uk/publications/2TS/calculators.asp
* Finishing pig performance (between 35kg and 110kg live weight): www.bpex.org/prices-facts-figures/costings/KPIFinishing.aspx
* Finishing pig management: www.thepigsite.com/pigjournal/articles/2169/management-practices-to-reduce-expensive-feed-wastage

Chapter 8:
Further reading and web/smartphone links:
www.bpex.org.uk/2TS/breeding
Practical Pig App – play.google.com and search BPEX Practical Pig.
Videos can also be downloaded at: practicalpig.bpex.org.uk
Essential further reading: *Nutrition of Sows and Boars* by W.H. Close and D.J.A. Cole, 2003.
Also advice for owners keeping pigs as pets or 'micro' pigs can be obtained from: www.rspca.org.uk and www.defra.gov.uk/ahvla-en/files/pub-pigs-micro-pet.pdf
How big do 'micro' pigs get: lancashiremicropigs.co.uk/how-big-do-micro-pigs-get-micro-pig-height-size-explained/
Why feeding kitchen waste is illegal: www.npa-uk.org.uk/disease.html?gclid=CLm60tPIwbkCFXQftAodDGQAvw

Chapter 9:
* Identification procedures: https://www.gov.uk/pigs-identification-registration-and-movement
* For pedigree registration download:
www.britishpigs.org.uk/recordingandID.pdf and also:
www.thepigsite.com/pighealth/article/561/identification-tattooing-slap-marking-tagging-etc
* Welfare: The UK Red Tractor Assurance Scheme includes a 'Real Welfare' assessment, including the confirmation that environmental enrichment objects are in use. See: www.bpex.org.uk/downloads/301028/298574/Environment%20Enrichment%20for%20Pigs.pdf
* Health issues:
www.thepigsite.com/diseaseinfo/
www.bpex.org.uk/2ts/health/FarmHealth/
www.pighealth.org.uk/phip/home.eb
www.bpex.org.uk/2TS/health/Bphs/default.aspx
www.porktraining.org/
'Pig Health and Welfare Council Annual Reports' via www.bpex.org.uk

www.thepigsite.com/diseaseinfo/41/erysipelas

CHAPTER REFERENCES

NOTIFIABLE DISEASES: KNOW THE SIGNS AND WHAT ACTION TO TAKE IF THERE IS A SUSPECTED CASE:
Links:
African Swine Fever (is also carried by 'soft ticks' (Ornithodorus))
www.defra.gov.uk/animal-diseases/a-z/african-swine-fever/
scotland.gov.uk/Topics/farmingrural/Agriculture/animal-welfare/Diseases/disease/african/signs

Swine Fever (CSF)
www.defra.gov.uk/ahvla-en/disease-control/notifiable/csf/
www.scotland.gov.uk/Topics/farmingrural/Agriculture/animal-welfare/Diseases/disease/fever/signs

Foot and mouth disease (affects cloven hoofed animals)
www.defra.gov.uk/ahvla-en/disease-control/notifiable/fmd/
www.scotland.gov.uk/Topics/farmingrural/Agriculture/animal-welfare/Diseases/disease/foot

Anthrax, Aujeszky's disease, Rabies, Swine vesicular disease etc.
www.defra.gov.uk/ahvla-en/disease-control/notifiable/

Chapter 10:
* Essential and useful information concerning showing and judging:
www.britishpigs.org.uk/shows.htm
www.nfyfc.org.uk/CompetitionsResources/ – see *Stockjudging guide – finished pig and pig carcase.*

* Animal movement regulations and procedures:
https://www.gov.uk/government/uploads/.../annexa-c-090713.pdf   and   https://www.gov.uk/.../uploads/.../pb13647-new-pig-keepers-guide.pdf

Further Reading

BOOKS

Brent, G., *The Pigman's Handbook of Problem Solving* (Crowood Press 2010).

Carr, J., *Garth Pig Stockmanship Standards* (5m Publishing 1998).

Close, W.H., and Cole, D.J.H., *Nutrition of Sows and Boars* (Nottingham University Press 2009).

English, Peter, *et al.*, *The Sow* (Farming Press Ltd 1982).

English, P., Burgess, G., Segundo, R., Dunne, J., *Stockmanship – Improving the Care of the Pig and Other Livestock* (Farming Press Books 1992).

Gadd, J., *Modern Pig Production Technology: A Practical Guide to Profit* (Nottingham University Press 2011)

Gadd, J., *Pig Production – What the Textbooks Don't Tell You* (Nottingham University Press 2005).

Gadd, J., *Pig Production Problems* (Nottingham University Press 2003).

Gibbs, J., *Pigs, Poultry and Poo – An Urbanite Couple's Journey to Country Life* (Crowood Press 2012).

Goldacre, B., *Bad Science* (Harper Collins 2008).

Hulsen, J., and Scheepens, K., *Pig Signals – Look, Think and Act* (Roodbont 2006).

McDonald-Brown, L., *Pigs for the Freezer – A Guide to Small Scale Production* (Crowood Press 2010).

Muirhead, M.R., Alexander, T.J.L., Carr, J., *Managing Pig Health* (5m Publishing 2013).

Smith, P., Bird, N., Crabtree, H.H., *Perfecting the Pig Environment* (Nottingham University Press 2009).

Smith, P., and Crabtree, H.H., *Pig Environment Problems* (Nottingham University Press 2005).

Stark, B.A., *et al.*, *Outdoor Pigs – Principles and Practice* (Chalcombe Publication 1990).

Thompson, J.E., Gill, P.G., Varley, M.A., *The Appliance of Pig Science* (Nottingham University Press 2004).

Thornton, Keith, *Practical Pig Production* (Farming Press Ltd 1981).

Thornton, Keith, *Outdoor Pig Production* (Farming Press Ltd 1988).

Varley, M., and Hughes, P., *Reproduction in the Pig* (Butterworth 1980).

White, M., *Pig Ailments, Recognition and Treatment* (Crowood Press 2005).

Whittemore, Colin T., *et al.*, *Whittemore's Science and Practice of Pig Production* (Blackwell 2006).

Wiseman, J., and Varley, M.A., *Perspectives in Pig Science* (Nottingham University Press 2004).

Wiseman, J., *The Pig – A British History* (Gerald Duckworth & Co. Ltd, 2nd revised edition, April 2000).

PERIODICALS AND ON-LINE PUBLICATIONS

Pig Farmer (on-line) BPEX on www.bpex.org.uk.

Pig Guide (hard copy and on-line) Reference guide to organisations and companies serving the UK pig industry, www.pig-guide.com.

Pig International (monthly on-line and hard copy), www.piginternational-digital.com.

International Pig Topics (monthly), PO Box 4, Driffield, Humberside Y025 9DJ, www.positiveaction.info/contact.php.

Pic Pig Improver, Fyfield Wick, Abingdon, Oxon OX13 5NA, www.pic.com.

Pig Progress (on line) International information www.pigprogress.net.

Pig & Poultry Marketing – Grove House www.farmbusiness.cc (hard copy and on-line).

Pig World (monthly) affiliated to the National Pig Association, published by Lewis Business Media, Suite A, Arun House, Office Village, River Way, Uckfield, East Sussex TN22 1SL, www.pig-world.co.uk/.

Practical Pigs (quarterly), produced in association with the BPA by Kelsey Publishing Goup, Cudham Tythe Barn, Berry's Hill, Cudham, Kent TN16 3AG.

The Pig Site (on-line) with a weekly newsletter and comprehensive on-line facilities, www.thepigsite.com.

Weekly Tribune (weekly electronic), subscription only publication for pig producers and the pig trade – published by Lewis Business Media, Suite A, Arun House, Office Village, River Way, Uckfield, East Sussex TN22 1SL, www.pig-world.co.uk/.

Relevant References:

Beynon, N.M., *Pig Marketing – Evaluation of Graded Market Outlets for Slaughter Pigs Using Micro-Processor Based Statistical Models*, thesis submission for the Warrant of the: C&G of London Institute Insignia Award in Technology, August, 1985.

Beynon, N.M., *Group Housing of Gestating Sows – Practical Examples from Various European Countries*, Leipziger Blaue Hefte Proceedings of the Leipzig Veterinary Surgeons' Congress, January, 2010.

Beynon, N.M., *Outdoor Pigs – Principles and Practice*, Chapter 8, 'Finishing Systems for Outdoor Pig Production', Chalcombe Publications, from a paper presented at Oxford University, 1989.

Beynon, N.M., Piglet Index: 'Useful measure of reproduction', *Pig International*, March/April, 2009, 22–23.

Beynon, N.M., 'Fostering Pigs: Essential management tool – How to manage the udder for higher numbers weaned', *Pig International*, May/June 2009, 22–23.

Bourne, S., and Taylor-Pickard, J.A., Alltech Inc.; Close, W.H., Close Consultancy; Beynon, N.M., N&R Services, 'Counting the cost of lost opportunities in Sow Production', *Pig Progress* Volume 29 No.3 2014.

Kauffold, J., Wehrend, A., Beynon, N., 'In the picture – Developments with ultrasonic scanning in pigs', *Pig International*, October 2010.

Kauffold, J., Althouse, G., Beynon, N., *Ultrasound Scanning – More than Just Pregnancy Testing*, Prairie Swine Centre, The Archives, July, 2011.

Kauffold, J., Rautenberg, T., Hoffman, G., Beynon, N., Schellenberg, I., Sobiraj, A., 'A field study into the appropriateness of transcutaneous ultrasonography in the diagnoses of uterine disorders in reproductively failed pig', *Theriogenology*, May 2005.

Glossary

ad libitum (ad lib) feeding the unrestricted supply of feed, day and night, usually in a dry form.

amino acids There are estimated to be twenty-two individual amino acids in pig meat protein. Ten of these are so-called essential AAs.

AssureWel A joint welfare assessment project for both sows and finishing pigs of the Soil Association, Bristol University and the RSPCA. www.assurewel.org/pigs

back fat The layer of fat usually related to that covering the loin area of the pig's back.

bacon The brine-cured meat from a pig carcase between 60 and 82kg.

baconer (UK) A class of finishing pig destined for bacon curing between 60 and 82kg carcase weight.

Blue pig The cross of pig resulting from, for example, a British Saddleback and a Landrace.

blue-ear pig disease *See* PRRS virus.

boar Any entire (uncastrated) male pig, normally kept for breeding purposes.

breeding herd The total inventory of gilts, sows, boars and suckling piglets.

carcase (carcass USA) The remains of the pig once the gut, pluck and so on are removed, leaving the head, trunk, backbone, feet and kidneys. The tongue is usually included, but an EEC regulation governs the weight adjustment if it is excluded.

casualty An emergency slaughter pig.

clean pigs Slaughter pigs that exclude entire males and mated or breeding females.

condition score A five- or ten-point scale designed to measure the degree of fat/body reserve in breeding females.

CPD Continuing Professional Development – *see* PIPR.

creep An area within the farrowing accommodation away from the sow constructed to provide warmth, protection and sometimes creep feed and/or milk substitute.

creep feed Feed designed to be fed to suckling piglets in the creep area.

dam The maternal parent, as used in pedigree records.

Doppler The principle of ultrasonics used in Doppler pregnancy testers.

dressed carcase weight The weight of a carcase once all internal organs and sometimes parts of the head have been removed.

Eliza Enzyme-linked immunosorbent assay, used in progesterone pregnancy-test kits and other rapid diagnosis methods.

empty days The number of days lost between weaning and effective service. This may include or exclude the five to seven days usually accepted as the normal weaning to service interval and comprises those days lost to each return to service (twenty-one days), abortions, or the days a barren sow remains in the herd prior to sale or death and replacement.

environmental enrichment Involves providing pigs with objects or substrates for proper investigation and manipulation to keep them occupied in non-harmful behaviour.

erysipelas Sometimes known as 'diamonds' when it occurs in the sub-acute form as skin blotches. The *Erysipelothrix* bacteria is believed to reside in the tonsils of around 50 per cent of all pigs. An economically damaging disease of turkeys. Can affect other animal species, including fish and reptiles.

fallen stock scheme A national service for the collection and disposal of fallen stock that helps farmers comply with the Animal By-Product Regulations (run by the NFSCo).

farrowing The birth of a litter of one or more live or dead pigs, normally occurring after the 111th day and before the 120th day after mating.

farrowing arc (also hut) A special outdoor pig hut designed for one sow or gilt to farrow and raise her litter. Designed to reduce the risk of crushing.

farrowing crate Specialized accommodation for the farrowing sow, designed to prevent crushing of piglets and the safe management of the sow.

farrowing index The average number of farrowings per sow per year in a herd. (It can have a different definition in some countries.)

farrowing interval The time, in days, between two consecutive farrowings for an individual sow. It is the sum of lactation length in days, days from weaning to successful AI or natural mating, and gestation length in days. 'Empty days' are included in this definition.

farrowing nest A free-access nest usually constructed of wood, which provides protection to the piglets and reduces crushing.

farrowing rate The percentage of sows which farrow to an AI or natural service, for example 86 per cent.

feed conversion ratio (FCR) The number of kilograms of feed required to increase live weight by one kilogram. Also FCE: farrowing conversion efficiency.

feeder (UK) Any pig from weaning to slaughter age. Also: feeding herd.

flat deck A form of nursery penning and housing for weaner pigs based on fully slatted flooring and supplementary heating.

Freedom Foods RSPCA farm assurance and food labelling scheme. www.freedom-food.co.uk/aboutus

full feeding Feeding pigs a given number of feeds a day, but attempting to satisfy their appetite on each occasion; also known as feeding to appetite.

gammon The cured or cooked hind leg – one of the most expensive cuts; in live pigs, the hind leg and ham region.

gestation The period of pregnancy measured in days between effective service and farrowing.

gilt Female pig that has not yet farrowed and reared her first litter.

gilt pool A group of maiden gilts awaiting service, to be used to replace culled sows.

heavy hogs (also heavy pig) Traditional class of slaughter pig usually weighing around 110 to 120kg (260lb) live when sent to the abattoir.

heritability (rate) The amount of a performance measure (trait) that is passed on from one generation to the next; back fat and carcase characteristics are highly heritable, whilst reproductive ones (litter size and so on) are not.

hog Castrated male pig.

hybrid vigour The superior performance of the offspring compared to the average performance of both parents. In pigs, the increase in numbers born is usually around 10 per cent.

kibble Coarsely ground or broken cereal grains.

killing out % The dressed carcase weight as a percentage of the live weight.

KPI Key Production Index, for example FCE, pigs reared per sow per year.

lactation The period of time during which the sow produces milk, starting at farrowing and normally ending at weaning.

lairage Pens at the abattoir where pigs are kept prior to slaughter.

litter scatter Percentage of litters with more than, or alternatively fewer than, a specified number of live born piglets (often used in computer-based graphical analysis).

liveweight gain The increase in weight between two weighings.

maiden gilt A young female pig, not yet mated for the first time.

maintenance The nutrient requirement of animals for the continuity of vital body processes.

mast Beech nuts and acorns foraged by fattening pigs during pannage. Germanic for fattening.

multiplier breeder A pig keeper who increases or multiplies hybrid, or pure-bred breeding stock for sale to commercial pig producers.

mummified piglets Dead piglets which are born in a discoloured or shrivelled state, because death occurred some time before farrowing and after around the thirty-fifth day of pregnancy.

mycotoxins These can contaminate feed and straw bedding and are a serious danger to young and breeding pigs. The Alltech 37+ Program can detect thirty-seven types of mycotoxin, including the known Fusarium and Fumonsins. Adding natural non-clay binders such as MycosorbA+ to the feed is very effective even against both feed storage mycotoxins.

nucleus breeder The pure-bred herd at the apex of a breeding pyramid, which attempts to improve the genetic merit and passes this on to the commercial producer directly or via a multiplier breeder or AI.

nursery Any specialized housing for the newly weaned pig, including bungalows, veranda units, flat decks and 'two-climate' weaner pens.

oestrous cycle (estrous USA) The twenty-one day (18–24) regulating hormonal cycle between oestrus periods (heats) in non-pregnant sows and gilts.

oestrus (estrus USA) The heat behaviour of females, during which the sow or gilt is receptive to mating by the boar.

oxytocin A hormone released from the pituitary gland at the base of the brain in response to stimulation of the udder, clitoris or cervix. It produces the milk let-down response and assists in contractions of the uterus and related muscles during birth and mating; it is available for injection in a 'natural' or in long-acting forms.

pannage The peasant's right to forage for mast in a landowner's forest, for example the New Forest (UK).

parity The number of times a sow has farrowed, including the expected farrowing.

parturition The act of farrowing.

PED virus Porcine edidemic diarrhoea (PED) – coronavirus pathogen – causing 80 to 100 per cent mortality in piglets in the USA in 2013.

piglet index A useful performance index based on the number of piglets born per 100 inseminations or sows naturally mated. This combines the farrowing rate (percentage) with the number of piglets born alive. A good piglet index would be 1,100 plus.

PIPR Pig Industry Professional Register – Register of the Continuing Professional Development (CPD) scheme for the pig industry – administered by City & Guilds Land-Based Services, formerly NPTC.

polyvalent vaccine A vaccine that covers a range of different serotypes of the same disease-causing organism.

porcine parvovirus A fertility-affecting virus causing the SMED (I) syndrome and found in over 50 per cent of the national herd.

pork Fresh pig meat.

porker A class of pig being finished for pork slaughter contracts at relatively light weights.

PRRS virus Porcine reproductive and respiratory syndrome virus disease.

prebiotics Stimulate growth and/or activity of bacteria in the digestive system in ways claimed to be beneficial to health. These include the oligosaccharide Alltech Actigen™ – this blocks the attachment of pathogenic bacteria to the gut wall, promoting the important lactobacillus bacteria.

probiotics Feed additives or oral products based on materials of microbial origin which can promote health and performance in animals. They are thought to do so by ensuring that the most beneficial populations of bacteria are in the digestive tract, and are mixtures of various organisms.

progeny testing Now almost universally replaced by performance testing. Involves testing the progeny of one sire and comparing their performance against the average of contemporary sires.

prolapse Either of the womb or rectum, which come outside the body due to weakened muscles or straining. They are both serious conditions.

prostaglandin One of several injectable products available to induce sows to farrow. This hormone switches off the progesterone-producing yellow bodies and triggers birth within twenty-five to thirty-five hours.

Real Welfare *See* Red Tractor and WOA for finishing pigs – a collaborative project between Red Tractor, BPEX and the University of Bristol. Also working with AssureWel.

Red Tractor Pig Scheme Aims to provide consumers and retailers with confidence regarding product quality attributes including food safety, animal welfare and environmental protection.

rescue decks Small piglet crèche facilities with milk replacer feeders to rescue piglets unable to suckle the sow adequately.

return to service A sow showing signs of mating usually around eighteen to twenty-four days from the last service.

rig A male pig with one testicle retained within the body.

runt Small, poorly developed pigs that can either be born small or get left behind due to inadequate nutrition.

rupture A weakness that allows part of the intestine to be forced either into the scrotum or from the navel (hernia).

scale feeding Feeding to a restricted level which is below appetite – usually 75 to 85 per cent of ad-lib appetite.

seedy cut Pigments in the mammary glands which cause discolouration in meat cuts. This tends to occur in coloured breeds and sexually mature gilts.

seminiferous tubules These grow to several kilometres in length in adult boars' testicles and produce up to a billion sperms in a thirty-five to forty-day cycle.

service A single act of mating or copulation; may be double or triple services.

sire The male or paternal father.

sounder Small social groups of wild boar ranging between six and thirty animals. This is usually a matriarchal group of a small number of sows and their recent offspring.

sow stall A restrictive form of individual penning. Now restricted and totally banned in several EU countries including the UK. It is only allowed for the first twenty-eight days of gestation in others.

suckler A piglet between birth and weaning.

Trobridge (monopitch pig housing) A registered trade name and a name used in many countries to describe a monopitch-roofed pig house for both finishing, grower, weaned pigs and sows.

two-ton sow or 2TS The name given to the UK initiative to increase the carcase weight sold by each sow each year. The target is to sell 2,000kg of pigs dead-weight per sow, and is equal to twenty-five pigs reared and sold and averaging 80kg at slaughter.

weaner A piglet permanently removed from the sow.

WOA Welfare Outcome Assessment is used to measure the welfare of animals on-farm – *see* 'AssureWel' and the 'Red Tractor' 'Real Welfare'; the 'Red Tractor' welfare outcomes project is collaboration between Red Tractor, BPEX and the University of Bristol.

www.bpex.org.uk/R-and-D/welfare/realwelfare.aspx

INDEX